As one of the world's longest established
and best-known travel brands,
Thomas Cook are the experts in travel.

For more than 135 years our
guidebooks have unlocked the secrets
of destinations around the world,
sharing with travellers a wealth of
experience and a passion for travel.

**Rely on Thomas Cook as your
travelling companion on your next trip
and benefit from our unique heritage.**

Thomas Cook **pocket** guides

# SANTORINI

Thomas
Cook

Your travelling companion since 1873

Written by Sean Sheehan, updated by Robin Gauldie

**Published by Thomas Cook Publishing**
A division of Thomas Cook Tour Operations Limited
Company registration no. 3772199 England
The Thomas Cook Business Park, Unit 9, Coningsby Road
Peterborough PE3 8SB, United Kingdom
Email: books@thomascook.com, Tel: + 44 (0)1733 416477
www.thomascookpublishing.com

**Produced by Cambridge Publishing Management Limited**
Burr Elm Court, Main Street, Caldecote CB23 7NU

ISBN: 978-1-84848-257-9

**First edition © 2008 Thomas Cook Publishing**
This second edition © 2010
Text © Thomas Cook Publishing
Maps © Thomas Cook Publishing/PCGraphics (UK) Limited

Series Editor: Adam Royal
Production/DTP: Steven Collins

Printed and bound in Spain by GraphyCems

Front cover photography © Thomas Cook

# CONTENTS

**INTRODUCTION**............................5
Getting to know Santorini...........8
The best of Santorini ...................12
Symbols key ....................................14

**RESORTS** .......................................15
Ia (Oia) ..............................................17
Kamari ...............................................27
Perissa ...............................................37
Thira (Fira).......................................47

**EXCURSIONS** ..............................57
Beach trips .......................................59
Island trips .......................................64
Inland trips.......................................67
Trips to neighbouring
  islands ...........................................77

**LIFESTYLE**....................................83
Food & drink....................................84
Menu decoder .................................92
Shopping...........................................95
Children.............................................98
Sports & activities .........................101
Festivals & events ..........................104

**PRACTICAL INFORMATION**....107
Accommodation ..............................108
Preparing to go................................112
During your stay ..............................116

**INDEX**............................................125

**MAPS**
Santorini ............................................6
Ia (Oia) ...............................................16
Kamari.................................................26
Perissa.................................................36
Thira....................................................48
Excursions..........................................58
Íos.........................................................78

## WHAT'S IN YOUR GUIDEBOOK?

**Independent authors** Impartial, up-to-date information from our travel experts who meticulously source local knowledge.

**Experience** Thomas Cook's 165 years in the travel industry and guidebook publishing enriches every word with expertise you can trust.

**Travel know-how** Thomas Cook has thousands of staff working around the globe, all living and breathing travel.

**Editors** Travel-publishing professionals, pulling everything together to craft a perfect blend of words, pictures, maps and design.

**You, the traveller** We deliver a practical, no-nonsense approach to information, geared to how you really use it.

**THE AUTHOR**

Sean Sheehan is a travel writer, living in Ireland. Greece is one of his favourite destinations, and he is also author of *The Illustrated Encyclopedia of Ancient Greece* (British Museum Press).

---

▶ *Blue and white defines Santorini's colour scheme*

# INTRODUCTION
Getting to know Santorini

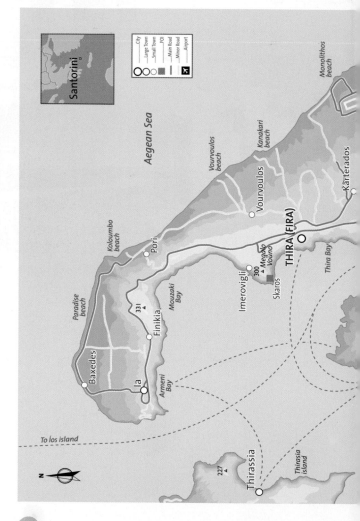

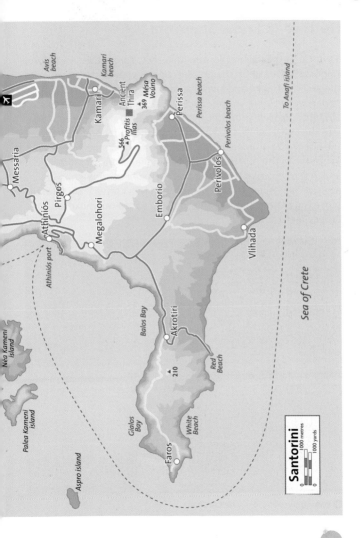

Avis beach

Kamari beach

Kamari

Ancient Thira

Mésa Vouno

369 ▲

Perissa

Perissa beach

Perivolos beach

566 ▲Profítis Ilías

Messaria

Pirgos

Athiniós

Athiniós port

Megalohori

Emborio

Perivolos

Vlihada

Nea Kameni island

Palea Kameni island

Aspro island

Balos Bay

Akrotiri

Red Beach

Gialos Bay

Faros

White Beach

210 ▲

To Anafi island

Sea of Crete

### Santorini

0 ___ 1000 metres
0 ___ 1000 yards

# Getting to know Santorini

Santorini is special and you are unlikely to forget the shapes and colours that make up the first sighting of your destination. From the air or sea, light and lines dazzle the eye and red-black cliffs tower over a cauldron-like space, which the sea filled after an almighty volcanic eruption around 1600 BC. The crater dropped into the sea, leaving its east rim above the water and forming the horseshoe-shaped main island that has become known as Santorini. To the northwest lies the smaller island of Thirasia and in the centre of the crater there is a pair of cone-shaped, even smaller islands, Palea Kameni and Néa Kameni. The overall scene is aesthetically arresting, making Santorini unlike any other Greek island.

🔺 *Reddish-purple volcanic rock in Thira*

## THE CYCLADES

Santorini is one of the Cyclades, a group of islands in the Aegean that derived its name ('circling') from the way the islands surround the sacred isle of Delos. The first inhabitants arrived from Asia Minor around 6000 BC but history proper begins 3,000 years later when an early Cycladic culture emerged. The Cyclades came under the influence of Crete, and Akrotiri on the island of Strongili – today's Santorini – became the most important cultural outpost of the advanced Minoan civilisation based on Crete. Then, suddenly and very violently, this came to a terrifyingly dramatic end with a huge volcanic eruption around 1600 BC.

### The volcano erupts

The eruption was an almighty one, affecting an estimated 150 billion tonnes of rock, and the collapse of the central part of the volcano created a large crater, a caldera, 22 sq km (8½ sq miles) in size and with a depth of up to 400 m (437 yards) below the existing sea level. As water rushed in to fill the vacuum a tsunami was created, moving southwards and overwhelming the shores of northern Crete with giant waves. Debris from the volcano covered an area of some 1,450 sq km (560 sq miles) and volcanic ash has been found on the ocean floor hundreds of miles from Strongili. What was left after the volcano had wrought its destruction was the archipelago of small islands, now called Santorini.

To what extent the eruption and resulting tsunami were responsible for the sudden end of Minoan civilisation, that occurred around but not exactly at the same time, remains a matter for conjecture. What is not contested is the fact that, when you look up at the cliffs from the sea on the western side of Santorini, the red, black, purple and brown colouring of the rock face is the living legacy of a colossal natural disaster that occurred over three-and-a-half thousand years ago.

## After the volcano

Material from the eruption, mostly ash, pumice and lava stones, created flat but fertile stretches of land on what remained of Strongili. This allowed life to resume and a new culture emerged in the 8th century BC after the arrival of Greek colonists. They called the main island Thira (Fira) and the name survived into the Byzantine era; in the 13th century it was conquered by the Venetians, who renamed it Santa Irene, giving it its modern name, Santorini. The largest of their forts still stands in the northwest of the island at Ia.

◯ *Thira harbour*

## TIMES CHANGE

Visitor-friendly, awash with bars and restaurants, and buzzing with nightlife both on the beaches and in the main settlement of Thira, Santorini has changed a lot since the massive eruption of ancient times. The lava flows that shaped the east coast also blessed it with volcanic sand, black in colour, that is astonishingly hot to touch in the heat of the day. The west coast summons holidaymakers to the edge of the crater for photogenic scenery and sunsets in a class of their own. The favourite spot for watching the sun go down is atop the volcano at the village of Ia. The east coast beaches are more hedonistic in character, while for secluded beaches and quieter scenes, the south coast beckons.

## ANCIENT PLEASURES

Going back to around 3000 BC, around 1,400 years before the volcanic eruption, Santorini was part of the advanced Bronze Age Minoan civilisation based in Crete. Perhaps the Minoans were drawn here by the quality of the island's *asyrtiko* grape; the dry, fresh wine that it makes is still one of the pleasures of island life. The remains of architecture from the Minoan age is still evident and there are museums displaying the unique finds that have been unearthed. A more sensual throwback to times past comes in the form of volcanic hot stone body massages.

## ATLANTIS

The suddenness of the volcanic eruption on Santorini and the destruction of its Minoan civilisation may have given rise to the myth of Atlantis, a lost wonderland that vanished in 24 hours. Santorini today has reinvented itself as a new Atlantis, a traveller's rest offering sunshine and beaches during the day, tavernas and conviviality at night, a stylish shopping scene and sophisticated food experiences.

# THE BEST OF SANTORINI

## TOP 10 ATTRACTIONS

- **The caldera** The volcano's summit exploded apart, creating a 22-sq-km (8½-sq-mile) crater that was flooded by the sea: the result, best viewed from Ia or from the road to Akrotiri, is a visually stunning land- and seascape that makes Santorini unique among the Greek islands (see page 17).

- **Ia (Oia)** Small, whitewashed dwellings and blue-domed churches hug the cliff face, higgledy-piggledy, in a warm fusion of colour and design. View the sunset from the remains of an old castle at the edge of town (see page 21).

- **Akrotiri** Take a walk down the street of a Minoan city buried since around 1600 BC when the volcanic eruption covered everything in lava (see page 71).

- **Perissa** A beach extending for 7 km (4¼ miles), a backdrop provided by the mountain Mésa Voúno, and a lively selection of bars and restaurants help make Perissa one of the island's favourite destinations (see page 37).

- **Kamari** A black beach too hot to walk on barefoot; dozens of bars and tavernas and a thousand sunbeds under the

shade of umbrellas make Kamari the epicentre of Santorini's beach life (see page 27).

- **Ancient Thira** The post-eruption city that emerged in the 9th century BC and an exhilarating, uphill walk from the beach at Perissa brings you to the terraced remains of the ancient city (see page 74).

- **Thira (Fira) nightlife** Bars and restaurants overlooking the crater, and music in nightclubs that stay open until the early hours (see page 54).

- **Boat trip to Palea Kameni** Volcanic, uninhabited islet with a burnt and alien landscape that bears testimony to the volcanic eruption; visits are served by easy-to-arrange day tours (see pages 59 and 65).

- **Local wine** Grapes grown without watering produce a wine unique to the island; the wineries, with guided tours and explanations of the production process, are open to visitors (see page 67).

- **Shopping in the narrow passageways in Ia and Thira** The most sophisticated shopping experiences, especially for jewellery, garments and galleries, and arts and crafts shops (see page 95).

▼ *The caldera seen from Thira*

## SYMBOLS KEY

The following symbols are used throughout this book:

ⓐ address ① telephone ① fax ⓦ website address ⓔ email
① opening times ① important

The following symbols are used on the maps:

| | | | |
|---|---|---|---|
| 𝒊 information office | | ○ | city |
| ✉ post office | | ○ | large town |
| 🛍 shopping | | ○ | small town |
| ✈ airport | | ■ | POI (point of interest) |
| ✚ hospital | | — | main road |
| 🛡 police station | | — | minor road |
| 🚌 bus station/stop | | | |
| ✝ church | | | |
| ❶ numbers denote featured cafés, restaurants & evening venues | | | |

### RESTAURANT CATEGORIES
The symbol after the name of each restaurant listed in this
guide indicates the price of a three-course meal for one
person excluding drinks
£= under €15    ££ = €15–30    £££ = over €30

① *Looking across the caldera from a small clifftop hotel, Thira*

# RESORTS
Places under the sun

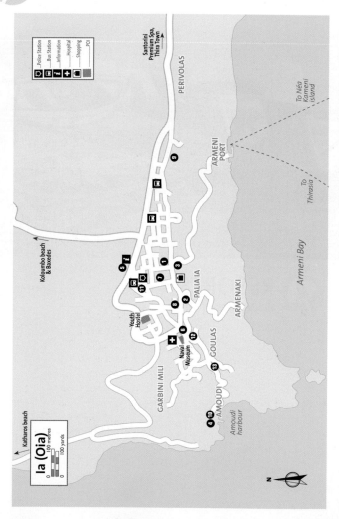

Ia (Oia)

0   100 metres
0   100 yards

Police Station
Bus Station
Information
Hospital
Shopping
POI

Koloumbo beach & Baxedes
Katharos beach
Santorini Premium Spa, Thira Town

PERIVOLAS
ARMENI PORT
To Nέa Kameni Island
To Thirasia
Armeni Bay
ARMENAKI
PALIA IA
ARMENI
GOULAS
AMOUDI
Amoudi harbour
GARBINI MILI
Youth Hostel
Naval Museum

N

# Ia (Oia)

The most picturesque of Santorini's resorts, Ia's charm lies in its unique and compact geography and its traditional, sculptured, pristine beauty. The village, tucked away on the northwest rim of the island just 11 km (7 miles) away from Thira, and looking down on the crater, was badly damaged by the 1956 earthquake but has been rebuilt and restored without losing its original attractiveness. Strict building regulations ensure that nothing unsightly disturbs lines of vision (no overhead electricity and telephone lines); and the residents, hoteliers and restaurateurs all appreciate the importance of preserving Ia's exquisite charm and air of calmness. A pedestrianised, clifftop walkway runs along the edge of the high ground, leading to the remains of an old Venetian fortress, and here you will find stylish bars, restaurants, cafés and shops lining your route. There are pathways that head off sideways but it is impossible to get lost.

There is a range of accommodation and, though bargains and budget places are rare, you can find in Ia (pronounced 'E-ah') some of the choicest places to stay anywhere on the island. Dwelling places cut into the rock face, once the private homes of sea captains, have been converted into boutique hotels and here, too, you will find some of the best restaurants on the island. Nor is there any shortage of quality places to drink and socialise; at dusk, the village becomes a magnet for holidaymakers from the east coast beaches seeking that perfect sunset. The views are stunning, whatever the time of day, and the blinding whiteness of the buildings against the darker colours of the rocky land and the deep blue of the Aegean – enhanced by a refined sense of the tasteful when it comes to exterior décor – provides a visual constant that makes the most casual of strolls into an aesthetic experience. Views of the volcanic islets and the larger island of Thirasia dominate the seascape.

Boat trips across the volcano submerged under the sea depart from the small port of Amoudi, which can be reached by a set of steps from Ia or by taking the paved road that leads down to the small bay. Here, too, are a couple of seaside tavernas where a drink and seafood can be enjoyed while watching the boats and, out at sea, the huge cruise ships that pass this way.

Being pedestrianised, the streets of Ia are wonderfully free from vehicle fumes and noise, but every day tourist coach parties come here and the town gets very busy. This is especially so as evening time approaches, because the sunsets are marketed as a mystical experience and viewing points close to the Venetian fortress and windmills attract many holidaymakers to watch the sun go down. The best time to view Ia and respond to its undeniable beauty is early in the morning, when the shops and galleries are beginning to open and the cafés have empty tables.

## BEACHES

The beaches close to Ia are not the main attraction of visiting this part of the island and consequently receive fewer visitors than those situated on the east and south coasts, which are more attractive and with better facilities. The closest one to Ia is **Katharos**, signposted on the road that leads down to Amoudi and being about 3 km (2 miles) away is within walking distance of the town. It is a pebbly beach, characterised by some rocky areas. Amoudi itself has a small rather stony beach, but there are good reasons for choosing not to swim or sunbathe here. The area is usually busy with boats, there is a danger of sudden swells caused by a cruise ship passing out at sea, and the depth drops so abruptly that it is not for inexperienced swimmers. The most visited beach is **Baxedes**, though it is rarely overfull. It has a stretch of black sand but because the water here deepens gradually, it is attractive to families, though not as good in this respect as Monolithos (see page 61). There are a couple of tavernas at Baxedes. The next beach, in the northwest of the island, is **Koloumbo**. You will need your own transport to get there and the final stretch to access its white pebbly terrain is by foot. Its isolation makes it suitable for nude sunbathing. There are no facilities here, though, so bring water and any food you need. Koloumbo and Baxedes are susceptible to strong winds coming in from the north, and when such winds are about there is little reason to stay at either beach for very long.

◔ *View of Ia from a boat trip*

## THINGS TO SEE & DO

### Naval Maritime Museum

Ia was once home to fishing families, with the better-off dwellings belonging to the relatively prosperous captains of commercial vessels, and this small museum, restored after the earthquake in 1956, is devoted to the town's maritime past. The history is richly documented from the 19th century onwards, in terms of photographs, vessels' figureheads, old seamen's chests and maritime equipment that includes a submarine's periscope.
ⓐ Main pedestrian street (bear right at the Y-junction at the Amoudi end of the street) ☏ 22860 71156 🕒 10.00–14.00, 17.00–20.00 Wed–Mon, closed Tues

### Santorini Premium Spa

A range of massage and skin care therapies, for males and females, whirlpool sessions, water therapy and a health bar stocked with health-renewing drinks and food. The spa is inside the Museum Spa Wellness Hotel and appointments can be booked online.
ⓐ Main pedestrian street ☏ 22860 71055
ⓦ www.santorinipremiumspa.com

### Shopping

Along with those in Thira, the shops in Ia undoubtedly offer the most sophisticated purchases to be made anywhere on the island. Souvenirs are available but not of the T-shirts and keyrings variety, and even the postcards here have a touch of class. The majority of shops are squeezed either side of the pedestrian route that leads along the top of the cliff from Perivolas, once a separate village, to the remains of the Venetian fortress at the end of the land. There are a number of quality jewellery outlets with prices that are clearly marked and fairly fixed. There are also some interesting boutiques with a small but appealing stock of fashionable garments for women (men are hardly catered for in Ia when it comes to clothing). Best of all are the art galleries retailing original works of art; the paintings and sculptures can be shipped home or wrapped securely as part of your luggage. There are also some enticing shops specialising in quality reproductions of ancient art.

## Watching the sunset

Cynics will tell you that the sunsets here are no better than those to be observed at Thira – an understandable reaction, perhaps, to the hype that has been built up surrounding the Ia phenomenon. However, the terminal point of high ground on the ramparts of the Venetian fortress offers a particularly clear line of sight towards the setting orb disappearing below the horizon to the west. The only drawback is that its reputation draws crowds and in high season there are just too many people in a limited space. Seeking that magical photograph can mean not being aware of coming perilously close to the edge, though if you are early enough to have a table at the café near the windmill, you can sit, sip and click in comfort for that special moment.

## TAKING A BREAK

### Bars & cafés

**Flora £ ❶** A pleasant cafeteria and pizzeria with tremendous views; ideal for a mid-morning break or an easy lunch with a leisurely drink. ⓐ Main pedestrian street ⓣ 22860 71424 ⓛ 09.00–22.00 daily

**Melevio £ ❷** A patisserie with sea views that will compete for your attention with the crêpes, pies, cakes, salads and traditional Greek desserts like *kataïfi* (a sweet pastry made with nuts) that make up the menu. This is an ideal spot for a light lunch. ⓐ Main pedestrian street ⓣ 22860 71149 ⓛ 09.00–19.30 daily

🔺 *Sunset over Ia*

**Skiza £** ❸  Views of the caldera and a terraced area to take in the panorama while munching on a waffle or pizza. Cakes and coffees add to the appeal of this eatery. ⓐ Main pedestrian street ❶ 22860 71569 ❹ 09.00–20.00 daily

**Sunset £** ❹  Often busy, you cannot be sure of finding a table, and reservations are not accepted. A favourite with locals for a plate of grilled octopus and a glass of *ouzo*. If full, try the adjoining taverna. ⓐ Amoudi ❶ 22860 71614 ❹ 09.00–21.00 daily

### Restaurants
**Edwin Polski Lokal £** ❺  Polish restaurant bar serving pizzas, grills and big choice of salads, omelettes and grills. Edwin is close to the main road but by evening time the coach runs are finished and it is not especially noisy. What it lacks in Ia refinement is compensated for by healthy prices and tasty food. ⓐ On the main road from Thira, just before the bus terminal ❶ 22860 71971 ❹ 13.00–24.00 daily

**Lotza £–££** ❻  At the western end of Ia's main street and commanding a stupendous view over the submerged volcano, this is an attractive restaurant for an evening meal. Starters like fried feta cheese in filo pastry with sesame seeds, lots of seafood like mussels, prawns and swordfish, and, for vegetarians, mixed vegetables with yogurt.
ⓐ Main pedestrian street ❶ 22860 71357 ❹ 09.00–22.00 daily

## AFTER DARK

### Restaurants
**Blue Sky ££** ❼  One of the friendliest places to enjoy an affordable meal in Ia, with a pleasant shaded area under a giant umbrella suitable for pre-dinner drinks. Fresh fish daily on the menu, traditional Greek dishes like *briam* (an oven-baked

vegetable casserole) and a 'summer salad' made from an appetising mix of rocket, mango and parmesan.
ⓐ Off Church Square ☏ 22860 71179 ⓦ www.bluesky-restaurant.gr ⏱ 08.00–24.00 daily

**1800 £££** ❽  This restaurant has a reputation as one of the very best places for an evening meal in Ia, so reservations are essential. The atmosphere strives to be romantic, with candlelit tables, but 1800 can become busier than you may desire.
ⓐ Main pedestrian street ☏ 22860 71485
⏱ 18.30–23.00 daily

**Canaves Ia £££** ❾  The restaurant is reached by taking the hotel's lift, or walking down 30 m (98 ft), to the poolside, where candlelit tables are laid out for a fine dining experience in a relaxing atmosphere. Reservations are essential, especially for one of the tables close to the cliff side. The hotel is close to the yellow-coloured church. ⓐ Main pedestrian street
☏ 22860 71453 ⓦ www.canaves.com ⏱ 19.30–22.00 daily

**Iliovasilena Amoudi £££** ❿  Old-fashioned fish restaurant on the quayside, where the catch comes straight from the boat to your table. ☏ 22860 71614 ⏱ 11.00–21.00 daily

**Kandouni £££** ⓫  Delicious meals like baked lamb with mustard sauce, herbs and baked potato stuffed with cheese. ⓐ Ia village
☏ 22860 71616 ⓦ www.kandouni.com ⏱ 16.00–01.00 daily

### Bars
**Meteor** ⓬  This rather natty bar has a few marble tables and chairs inside the bar area, with glimpses of the sea across a tiny balcony, and more tables across the street under a canopy. Cocktails and coffees, home-made ice cream and snacks, Greek micro-brewed beer on draught – with cool jazz music in the

background – help make Meteor one of the most relaxing places to while away the late hours. ⓐ Main pedestrian street ❶ 22860 71015 ⏱ 08.00–02.00 daily

**Sun Spirit** ⓭ Café and bar at Ia's terminal point, between the ruins of the Venetian fortress and Golden Sunset Villas and its windmill, this is a prime spot for watching the sun go down while sipping a drink. ⓐ Main pedestrian street ❶ 22860 45689 ⓦ www.sunspirit.gr ⏱ 09.00–01.00 daily

⬤ *Ia sits on a clifftop*

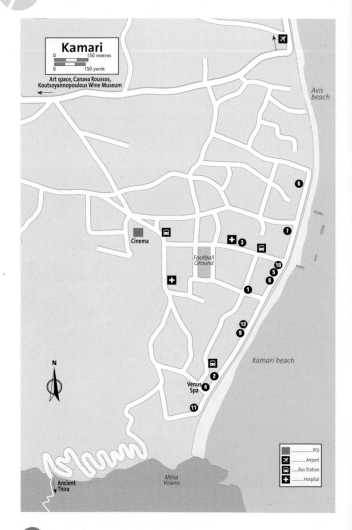

Kamari

0 ——— 150 metres
0 ——— 150 yards

Art space, Canava Roussos,
Koutsoyannopoulous Wine Museum

Avis beach

Cinema

Football Ground

Kamari beach

N

Venus Spa

Mésa Vouno

Ancient Thira

POI
Airport
Bus Station
Hospital

# Kamari

Kamari, on the east coast, vies with Perissa as the island's most popular beach resort, and it soon becomes apparent why this is the case. Its beach of pebbles and black sand is filled with sunbeds and umbrellas and there is a concentrated 2-km (1¼-mile) long strip of hotels, restaurants, bars, nightclubs and shops forming the heart of the resort. Behind this main drag there are a number of smaller streets with more restaurants, bars and shops. With an open-air cinema within walking distance and a number of wineries close by, plus watersports and spas, Kamari has a lot to offer and there is no other resort on Santorini with such a wide choice when it comes to accommodation, places to eat and organised activities. A road from the southern end leads to ancient Thira (see page 74), atop Mésa Voúno, a reminder of the fact that Kamari was the port of the ancient city. The earthquake of 1956 damaged Kamari, and what you see today is largely the result of building work over recent decades. There is little sense of Kamari as a Greek village of the traditional kind but nor does it suffer from high-rise hotel blocks; its holiday appeal defines its presence and character and this makes it a convenient and appealing base for a holiday on Santorini.

Parallel to the pedestrianised beach walkway runs a regular street where ATMs and the bus stops are found. There is a service to and from Thira, departing every half hour 08.30–23.00 daily (and an early bus departing at 07.30). Buses also run regularly on a daily basis to Imerovigli and Ia. Taxis are easy to find but you should agree on the fare beforehand. At the northern end of the main traffic street there is a modern shopping centre with shops and a cinema. Kamari does not close down completely over winter; the cinema here stays open, as do some of the restaurants and bars. Indeed, a sure guide to the best places for a meal are those that do stay open all year and rely on local customers as well as tourists.

Kamari's long beach is filled with loungers and sun umbrellas

Given Kamari's hotspot status, there is no shortage of tour operators and travel agents, and this makes it an ideal base for organising excursions and trips to other islands. It is worth comparing prices and packages, although rates are fairly standard and offer more or less the same level of service. See, for example, ⓦ www.kamaritours.gr. There is also a large number of places hiring out vehicles and plenty of shops with internet access. You will also find places where you can download your digital pictures onto CD, to free up space on your camera.

The main church of Panagia Episkopi, just outside Kamari, is worth reaching if you are around on 15 August. The church celebrates the feast of the Virgin Mary on that day and a festival air prevails. Similarly, on 24 September check out the Panagia Mirtidiotissa church for another feast day that is celebrated by locals, with food and wine.

## BEACHES

Kamari beach is pebbly but safe for swimming. Its Blue Flag status guarantees water quality, but above the tideline the sand can be somewhat littered by the end of the summer; for reassurance, swim within clear sight of the lifeguard's post. The beach is characterised by the looming presence of Mésa Voúno at its southern end. Kamari's long and straight strip of black sand is accompanied every inch of the way on dry land by shops, restaurants and bars.

Kamari's tourist infrastructure and abundance of hotels makes it a first choice with tour operators yet, despite the large numbers of holidaymakers, this beach resort manages to retain an air of civilised hedonism. The main walkway that runs parallel with the beach is not open to vehicles and this adds enormously to the appeal of Kamari. There are nightclubs and bars that remain lively until early morning but accommodation is mostly set back from the beach area, so the late-night social scene does not intrude on anyone seeking a quieter time after dark. The beach is close to the airport and sunbathers can clearly see, and hear, flights arriving and departing throughout the day.

The southern end of the beach is blocked by a huge rocky headland, Mésa Voúno, close to which a water taxi takes passengers around it to neighbouring Perissa (see page 37). Northwards, the beach extends as far as Monolithos (see page 61). The beach itself is well organised and the sunbeds can be rented by the day or used by customers of the bars and restaurants that have their own allocation, usually clearly demarcated by colour. By the middle of August you will need to arrive on the beach after breakfast to secure a sunbed. Nearly all the small lanes running off the pedestrianised walkway lead to hotels and pensions as well as more shops and restaurants. At some stage of your stay, you will find the need to get off the beach and explore some of the byways and at night, if seeking a quieter place for a drink or a meal, walk to either end of the beach and head inland.

## THINGS TO SEE & DO

### Art Space

An underground art gallery and a guided tour devoted to the wine culture and production process on Santorini. Bottles of wine and grappa for purchase, small enough to fit into checked-in luggage, are securely wrapped.

ⓐ Exo Gonia. Signposted on the left, if travelling on the road towards Messaria from Kamari, just before the turning left to Pirgos ⓣ 22860 32774 ⓦ www.artspace-santorini.com ⓛ 11.00–sunset daily ⓘ Admission charge

## Beach watersports

Water-skis, wakeboards, kiteboards and boats for rental as well as windsurfing lessons and rental from 3sxsport+fun.

ⓐ Kamari beach ❶ 6932 780852 Ⓦ www.3sxsport.gr
🕒 08.30–19.00 daily

## Canava Roussos

The oldest winery on Santorini, now in its fourth generation, producing eight types of wine – all or some of which can be tasted in a pleasant, outdoor area overhung with vine leaves. The short, guided tour of the winery is free but there is a charge for the wine-tasting.

ⓐ Main Street, Episkopi. Signposted on the left, if travelling on the road towards Messaria from Kamari ❶ 22860 31278
Ⓦ www.canavaroussos.gr 🕒 11.00–20.00 daily (June–Sept); 11.00–19.00 daily (May & Oct), closed Nov–Apr

## Koutsoyannopoulos Wine Museum

The museum, part of Volcan Wines' winery, is 6 m (20 ft) underground and runs for a length of 300 m (984 ft). The history of wine and the life story of a Santorini wine producer are told by way of models and sound effects. Visitors make their own way around the museum with an audio guide (available in different languages). There is a large bar area where wine-tasting takes place.

ⓐ Signposted on the right if travelling on the road towards Messaria from Kamari ❶ 22860 31322 Ⓦ www.volcanwines.gr
🕒 12.00–20.00 daily (Apr–Nov); 09.00–14.30 Mon–Sat (Nov–Mar) ❶ Admission charge and separate charge for the wine-tasting

## Open-air cinema

It takes about half an hour to walk from the beach to Kamari's open-air cinema for the novel experience of simultaneously watching a movie under the stars and feeling the warm evening breeze.

**ⓐ** Take the main road out of the resort and it is on the left (look for the reproduction of an old projector outside the cinema, where trees begin to line the road) **ⓣ** 22860 31974
**ⓦ** www.cinekamari.gr

### Venus Spa

One-, two-, three- and four-day programmes, plus a wide range of face, body, and hand and feet treatments for men and women. There is a hydrotherapy, as well as a Turkish, bath and 'self-healing' marine mud, as well as regular body massages.
**ⓐ** Venus Afroditi Hotel **ⓣ** 22860 32760
**ⓦ** www.afroditivenushotel.gr

## TAKING A BREAK

### Bars & cafés

**Aegean Café £ ❶** This Irish-style pub offers satellite television for football and other sports, and familiar draught beers. Free internet use for customers. **ⓐ** First street inland and parallel to Kamari beach **ⓣ** 22860 33850 **ⓦ** www.aegeancafe.gr
**ⓛ** 10.00–24.00 daily

**Pasta Fresca £ ❷** A bar and restaurant, so you might drop by for a drink and end up ordering one of the menu specials: pizza, ravioli, tagliatelle and gnocchi. **ⓐ** Sunshine Hotel, Kamari beach
**ⓣ** 22860 31007 **ⓦ** www.hotelsunshine.gr **ⓛ** 08.00–02.00 daily

### Restaurants

**Casa Kamari £ ❸** The food is an agreeable mixture of Greek and Mediterranean and the atmosphere is pleasingly restrained.
**ⓐ** Atlantis Shopping Centre **ⓣ** 22860 32140
**ⓦ** www.casakamarirestaurant.com **ⓛ** 08.30–23.00 daily

◔ *Looking down over Kamari*

**THE BEST ON THE BEACH**
The two best restaurants on Kamari beach stand next to one another, Nuxtépi and Classico Café, evidenced by the fact that both establishments remain open after most tourist-oriented places have closed for the season; native islanders travel here to enjoy typically Greek and Mediterranean-style dishes cooked with expertise.

**Remy £–££** ❹ Daily lunch specials like a Greek salad and a beer, or spaghetti with pesto and a soft drink, at budget prices. A more substantial fill could be enjoyed by way of lamb chops with mint sauce or a veal fillet and fennel. ⓐ Kamari beach ❶ 22860 33224 ⏱ 08.30–23.00 daily

**Classico Café ££** ❺ Arrive here for lunch and you may well be tempted to return for an evening meal. The house salad should be tasted, and so should the home-made ice creams (try the one that uses *mastika* from Chios); carnivores will love the steaks from Argentina and the lamb cooked in herbs with vine leaves. ⓐ Kamari beach ❶ 22860 23112 ⓦ www.santorini-classico.gr ⏱ 08.30–23.00 daily

## AFTER DARK

### Restaurants
**Almira £–££** ❻ Walking northwards, Almira is almost the last restaurant before the big rock, but it is worth the journey because this friendly place has a good menu of appetisers like *taramasalata* (fish roe), *fava* (yellow split peas), artichokes with feta, and a range of grilled dishes. The seafood is good and vegetarians should have no problem finding something to enjoy. There is also a children's menu. ⓐ Kamari beach ❶ 22860 33477 ⏱ 08.30–24.00 daily

**Syrtaki £–££** ❼ Various specials, like pork chops with a Greek salad, make Syrtaki an economical place to eat; especially so for two people because the menu lists various options priced for sharing couples. ⓐ Kamari beach ❸ 22860 32777 ⓦ www.syrtaki-santorini.gr ⓛ 10.00–24.00 daily

**Nichteri ££–£££** ❽ The Cyprus salad is a delicious mix of figs and haloumi cheese and the *meze* include the island's *fava* and white aubergine as well as shrimps *saganaki* (tomato sauce and feta cheese) and a superb octopus in red wine sauce. The grilled seafood, like *brantada* (cod) or lobster spaghetti, are the big draw when it comes to a main dish. ⓐ Kamari beach ❸ 22860 33480 ⓦ www.nichteri.gr ⓛ 12.00–24.00 daily

### Bars & clubs
**Albatross Club** ❾ Happy hour from 20.00 until 23.00 and then the dance floor livens up; no cover charge and good DJs. ⓐ Kamari beach ❸ 22860 31657 ⓛ 20.00–03.00 daily

**Dom** ❿ Currently the most popular nightclub in Kamari and always packed with partygoers. ⓐ Kamari beach ❸ 22860 33420 ⓛ 20.00–03.00 daily

**Hook Bar** ⓫ Almost the last bar at the southern end of the beach, this colourful, flower-draped bar has an inviting décor and the music – oldies from the 1960s and 70s – attracts a regular crowd of devotees, nightly. ⓐ Kamari beach ❸ 22860 33441 ⓛ 08.00–02.00 daily

**Oxygen** ⓬ By day, Oxygen is a quiet, bright and cheerful bar, but after dark it transforms into one of the resort's favourite destinations. Happy hour from 19.00, plus good, healthy food served all day. ⓐ Kamari beach ❸ 22860 31711 ⓛ 11.00–04.00 daily

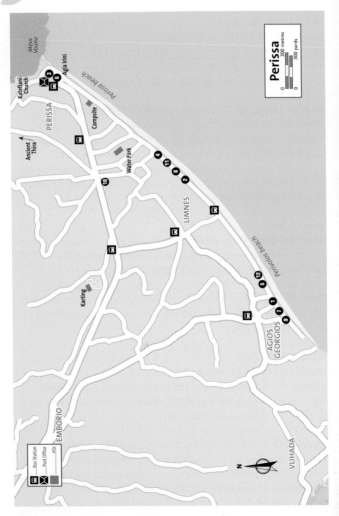

## Perissa

Perissa is in the southeast of Santorini, 13 km (8 miles) from
Thira, and is home to the two main beaches of Perissa and
Perivolos, with a small neighbourhood in between called
Limnes. There is a quieter stretch of beach towards the
southwest, called Agios Georgios (St George) and then a
relatively isolated stretch of sand before reaching Vlihada.

In general, Perissa beach – its northern end at least – tends
to attract older couples while the more sports-oriented
holidaymaker will tend to be drawn towards the other end of
the beach, the section approaching Perivolos. The bars towards
the Perivolos end have louder music and team sports like
volleyball are organised on the beach itself. Due to the
combined length of Perissa and Perivolos, some 7 km (4¼ miles)
in all, it is a long walk between the two and would take
45 minutes to an hour to stroll from one end to the other.
The road that runs parallel to the beach is open to traffic,
so if you have a hired vehicle there is no problem in getting
about. The advantage of the long distance, on the other
hand, is that you can head off for an evening walk after the
heat of the day and discover somewhere new to enjoy a meal
or drink.

Perissa has a plethora of affordable and budget places to stay,
including a campsite and a hostel, and this draws in a young set.
While this makes for a loud and sociable atmosphere in some of
the bars, there are also some very smart hotels in which to base
oneself, like the Meltemi Luxury Suites (see page 111). Places like
this have their own pools and you can sunbathe or dawdle away
the hottest part of the day before heading down to the beach
bars and restaurants as dusk approaches.

A short and easily walked distance away from the beach road
there is the main road that connects Perissa with Emborio, and
here you will find some quieter bars and restaurants. Emborio

itself is a large village and its name, which comes from the Greek word for 'trade', suggests it was once a commercial centre. Nowadays, though, commerce is very much at the heart of Perissa and it would be easy to base yourself here for an extended stay, with occasional excursions to other parts of the island.

Given the popularity of Perissa as a sun-and-sand destination, it does become very crowded in July and August, but this tends more to be the case along the main strip that ends at the northern end of the beach. For a quieter experience, it would probably be wiser to keep to the Perivolos end and there are some relatively laid-back bars and restaurants here. Along the busiest part of Perissa there are some restaurants – the kind where potential customers are importuned a tad too earnestly – that are best avoided.

## BEACHES

### Agios Georgios
Other than the paved road coming to an abrupt end, the dividing line between the beach of Agios Georgios and that of Perivolos has no more of a natural marker than the division between Perivolos and Perissa. The human landscape, however, changes perceptibly because far fewer people make the effort to come this far. There are no organised watersports and the further south you walk the fewer people you will encounter.

### Perissa
Were it not for the rocky headland of Mésa Voúno, the beach at Perissa would simply be the continuation southwards of Kamari's beach. It is the same kind of black sand and it is very long. This has given plenty of scope for visitor-orientated developments and you will certainly not have a problem finding somewhere to eat or drink. The northern end of the beach has

the greatest concentration of bars and restaurants and this, too, is where the boat taxi to and from Kamari stops. The backdrop of mountains makes Perissa beach the one best protected from summer winds from the Aegean.

## Perivolos
Southwestwards along Perissa's beach, towards Perivolos, there is a stretch of fairly empty sand, a kind of holidaymaker's no-man's land. Due to a relative dearth of bars and restaurants, this stretch of beach has fewer pockets of sunbeds laid out on the sand and this makes it suitable for people who want a bit of space around them. After this stretch of relative emptiness, the beach scene livens up again with another burst of bars and places to eat, and this section of beach – which is a natural extension of Perissa, towards Agios Georgios – is Perivolos. It is a well-organised beach with plenty of watersports, like waterskiing and windsurfing. ❶ 22860 81512
Ⓦ www.wavesports.gr

## Vlihada
This is not one of the most populated beaches on Santorini, but it is certainly one of the most attractive, and if you are walking here from Perivolos you will come across some quite isolated stretches of sand where nude bathing will not attract undue attention from others on the beach.

## THINGS TO SEE & DO

### Agia Irini
The typically blue-coloured domes of this photogenic church make it a sight difficult to miss at the northern end of Perissa beach. There is little of interest inside the church, but its exterior is dramatic in an understated way, standing as it does beneath the huge rock that dwarfs it.

🔼 *Blue domes on Agia Irini church*

## Panagia Katefiani

It is difficult not to notice this small church from Perissa, perched in a natural niche high up in Mésa Voúno, because it is impossible not to find yourself gazing up at the huge rock and wondering how a building ever got to be built there. It takes about half an hour to walk to the church from the northern end of Perissa beach. Follow the signs to ancient Thira and after walking uphill for about ten minutes you will see a white arrow, painted on a rock, pointing to the right. A visit to the church could be part of a longer walk to ancient Thira (see below and page 74).

## Santorini Water Park

Three swimming pools and sunbeds and umbrellas for 180 people, plus three water slides, two bars and a restaurant. Popular with families – there is a pool and a water slide for children – this is not the place to come for a quiet sunbathe with a good book, but for fun and a lively atmosphere it is hard to beat.

ⓐ Perissa beach ❶ 22860 81118 Ⓦ www.santoriniwaterpark.gr
🕙 10.00–24.00 daily ❶ Admission charge (pools close at 19.00)

## Walk to ancient Thira

It takes less than an hour to reach the site of ancient Thira, atop Mésa Voúno, from ground level at the northern tip of Perissa beach. Follow the sign to ancient Thira and take the footpath that heads up the side of the hill. The walk is fine for anyone with a basic level of fitness but bring plenty of water, and some kind of headgear might be helpful to keep the sun off your neck and face. To avoid heat exhaustion this walk is best undertaken early in the morning or early evening time. It is an uphill route all the way but never becomes gruelling and there are great views of Perissa and Kamari when you reach the top.

## Wave sports

Most watersports are catered for, including parasailing, jet- and waterskiing, wakeboarding and windsurfing. A variety of water vessels, like canoes, kayaks and sea bicycles, are available for hire and diving trips can be arranged.

ⓐ Perivolos beach, attached to Chili Beach Bar, and Perissa beach in front of the Atlantis Island restaurant ❶ 22860 81512 ⓦ www.wavesports.gr

## Yolanda Liva

Massages arranged and booked through your accommodation tend to be pricey because the hotel adds its own commission. Yolanda Liva is an independent operation and rates are more attractive. Thai-style massages, lasting an hour or 90 minutes, are available as are 30-minute back or face-and-head massages.

ⓐ Perissa ❶ 6949 153369/6944 506906

## TAKING A BREAK

There are three outstanding Perissa restaurants: Lava for traditional Greek, The Nets (Ta Dihtia) for seafood and Sea Side for chic Mediterranean.

### Bars & cafés

**Cayo £ ❶** Visually stunning interior – blindingly white – makes this possibly the most stylish watering hole on either Perissa or Perivolos beach. Some 20 types of coffee are available plus a range of sandwiches and non-meat options such as vegetable tart or aubergines with mozzarella and tomatoes. All against a background of non-stop music. ⓐ Perivolos beach ❶ 22860 81821 ❶ 08.30–22.30 daily

**Perissa Bay Bar £ ❷** This friendly bar, part of the Perissa Bay hotel, has a good menu of omelettes, pizzas, smoothies and

Sumptuous views from ancient Thira

waffles with ice cream. Check any special meals on the blackboard. If you decide to return in the evening, happy hour is 18.00–22.00. ⓐ Limnes, Perissa beach ⓣ 22860 81970 ⓦ www.perissabay.com ⓛ 08.00–late daily

## Restaurants
**Aquarius ££** ❸ One of the largest restaurants in Perissa; certainly the largest menu: snacks, salads, pasta, pizza, Greek, grills and seafood. A takeaway service with free delivery is an option but the tables by the beach are inviting. ⓐ Perissa beach ⓣ 22860 82109 ⓦ www.aquarius-santorini.com ⓛ 08.30–23.30 daily

**Atlantis ££** ❹ Immaculately clean restaurant that is a hybrid between a taverna, a pizzeria and a smart restaurant. Prices are competitive and at the bottom end of the **££** category if you like pizza. ⓐ Perissa beach ⓣ 22860 81473 ⓛ 09.00–22.30 daily

## AFTER DARK

## Restaurants
**Meteora £–££** ❺ Perhaps the best of the more populist type of restaurant of which Perissa has so many. Monday nights have a Greek theme, with live music and a gregarious atmosphere. The menu is huge in scope and non-carnivores will find items like *papoutsakia* (stuffed aubergine and vegetables). ⓐ Perivolos beach ⓣ 22860 82777 ⓛ 10.00–23.00 daily

**Porto Castello £–££** ❻ Unashamedly touristy, come here on a Friday night for a lively Greek theme with dancers. There are tables inside as well as ones almost touching the beach; also a roof garden area. ⓐ Perissa beach ⓣ 22860 82829 ⓦ www.portocastellosantorini.com ⓛ 10.00–23.00 daily

**Ta Dihtia ££ ❼** A superb fish tavern, worth the trek to this end of the beach. One of the house specialities is an appetiser of cuttlefish cooked in its own ink with cracked wheat and fennel. Equally good is the *bekri meze* (squid, cuttlefish, octopus, shrimp and hot peppers). Vegetarians should try the smoked aubergine with garlic, balsamic vinegar and parsley. ⓐ Agios Georgios, Perivolos beach ❶ 22860 82818 ⓛ 10.00–23.00 daily

**Lava ££ ❽** Tradition rules OK at Lava, and customers are shown the food in the kitchen area. Meat dishes in tasty sauces and plenty of choice, like peppers stuffed with cheese or, for vegetarians, wheat and melted sesame. Brown bread, too, is always served. ⓐ Limnes, Perissa beach ❶ 22860 81776 ⓛ 09.00–23.00 daily

**Sea Side ££ ❾** Excellent dips, mussels, prawn with caper leaves, tuna *carpaccio* and quality meat dishes. Sea Side could be the coolest place in Perissa for contemporary Mediterranean food and a laid-back mood. There is one special table on the beach for romantics, but reserve in advance. ⓐ Agios Georgios beach ❶ 22860 82801 ⓦ www.notos-restaurant.gr ⓛ 10.00–23.00 daily

### Bars & clubs

**Dorians ❿** Claiming to be the oldest bar in Perissa, this is one of the most pleasant bars not actually on the beach. The palm tree setting provides natural shade and with music from the 1960s and 70s, Dorians is popular with visitors who crave nostalgia. British holidaymakers love this place and the beer is very competitively priced. ⓐ Main road, Perissa ❶ 22860 81744 ⓛ 11.00–24.00 daily

**Question Mark Beer House ⓫** The stereotypical beach bar: look for the old jeeps mounted on plinths outside or listen out for the DJ-driven loud music that blasts out nightly. Claims to have

70 different kinds of beer. ⓐ Limnes, Perissa beach
ⓣ 6977 668915 ⓛ 10.00–late daily

**Sea View** ⓬ Next to, and under the same management as, the
Meteora restaurant, Sea View has a quiz night on Thursdays and
karaoke on Saturdays. For Premier League football there is a
large screen. ⓐ Perivolos beach ⓣ 22860 82777
ⓛ 10.00–24.00 daily

🔺 *The northern end of Perissa beach*

# Thira (Fira)

Thira is the administrative capital of Santorini and, with about 3,000 residents, the largest centre of population on the island. Although Thira has no beaches, the island is small enough to make the town your home base for at least a couple of days, if not longer, with day trips to the east, south or north for the sun-drenched, sandy beaches. If your accommodation is beach-based, be sure to make at least one visit to Thira. The town has plenty to offer and see, and here you will find many of the island's best restaurants, Santorini's two noted museums, sophisticated shops, cosy bars and a surprisingly lively nightlife. Best of all, Thira is like Ia in being perched on the rim of the volcano, 260 m (853 ft) above sea level, and there are jaw-dropping views of the island-studded sea and the towering cliffs. The town was badly damaged by the earthquake of 1956 and large sections of it had to be completely rebuilt. This resulted in patches of poorly designed buildings but, fortunately, the stepped walkway, Agiou Mina, has preserved a sense of the past. It affords visitors unbeatable views from the light-filled verandas of the boutique hotels, bars and restaurants that discreetly pepper the route.

Cruise ships anchor out at sea and bring their passengers to a tiny port below Thira, from where mules and donkeys carry them up a winding set of steps. If your lodgings are close to the cliffs, the silence of the morning will be fractured by the tinkling bells of the mules making their way down to the port for the early arrivals. There is also a cable car between the port and the town for those who don't fancy the donkey ride.

The only drawback to Thira is that, especially in July and August, the narrow cobbled streets become overcrowded with visitors. The buses that travel to and from Akrotiri, the main port of Órmos Athiniós, Monolithos, the airport, Vlihada, Perissa, Kamari, Baxedes and Ia run frequently on a daily basis but are

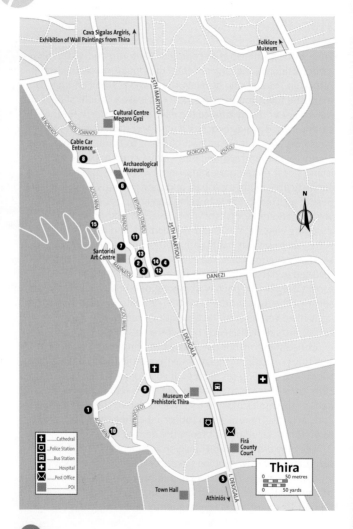

Cava Sigalas Argiris,
Exhibition of Wall Paintings from Thira

Folklore
Museum

25TH MARTIOU

M NOMIKOU

AGIOU IOANNOU

Cultural Centre
Megaro Gyzi

Cable Car
Entrance
**8**

GEORGIOUS KOLSOU

Archaeological
Museum
**6**

AGIOU MINA

FEITHIOU STAVROU

IPAROUS

**15**

**7**

**11**

Santorini
Art Centre

**13**

**2**

**3**

**14**

**12**

**4**

25TH MARTIOU

MARINATOU

DANEZI

I. DEKIGALA

✝

**9**

Museum of
Prehistoric Thira

🚔

✉

Firá
County
Court

**1**

MITROPOLEOS

**10**

AGIOU MINA

Town Hall

**5**

Athiniós ▾

I. DEKIGALA

N

| ✝ | .....Cathedral |
| 🛡 | ...Police Station |
| 🚌 | .....Bus Station |
| ✚ | .....Hospital |
| ✉ | .....Post Office |
| | .....POI |

**Thira**

| 0 | 50 metres |
| 0 | 50 yards |

usually packed. They depart from and arrive at an area just south of Plateia Theotokopoulou, opposite the Museum of Prehistoric Thira. This is also the main area for picking up a taxi or being deposited by one if you arrive from the east or north coast. The time to try to avoid the crowds, apart from being here out of season, is early in the morning or during the mid-afternoon. Best of all is a late-night stroll through the walkways and cobbled streets for Thira, like the whole island, is a remarkably safe place to wander through. When the hubbub has faded away, there are small bars and cafés along the clifftop, and even at night the pristine whiteness of the buildings makes itself felt and a peaceful atmosphere pervades the scene.

## THINGS TO SEE & DO

### Archaeological Museum

Situated close to the cable car entrance, the museum is home to artefacts excavated at ancient Thira on Mésa Voúno. The collection is not too extensive and there is time to take in everything on a single visit. There are also some examples of red and black vases from around the 5th century BC, the Classical period, but it is the frescoes that will catch your attention. The sculptures on show are mostly from the later Hellenistic period.
ⓐ Ipapadis ⓣ 22860 22217 ⓦ www.culture.gr ⓛ 08.30–20.00 Tues–Sun, closed Mon ⓘ Admission charge

### Cable car & mule rides

The cable car connects the town of Thira with the small port of Skála Firás and, unless you are arriving on a cruise ship, there is no necessity to use this mode of transport. It is, though, a short and dramatic trip and just for the fun of being hoisted up or down the cliff face of an extinct volcano you may want to take the cable car one way and then either a ride by mule or a none-too-exacting walk of 580 snake-like steps.

⬥ An aerial view of Thira

🕐 Cable car every 20 minutes 06.40–22.00 daily (May–Oct); mule ride fixed charge

### Cava Sigalas Argiris
This place is regarded by some as the producer of Santorini's finest wines; judge for yourself by tasting their wines. A visit here also allows you to make purchases of local food products like caper leaves, dried chickpeas and tomatoes. The winery is at Firostefani, a little way out of Thira on the road to Ia, and there are great views of the caldera from here.
ⓐ Firostefani ☎ 22860 22802 🕐 09.00–17.00 daily

### Exhibition of Wall Paintings from Thira
The reason for walking north out of town to this conference centre is to view the life-size reproductions of all the wall paintings from Akrotiri. The most important originals have ended up in the National Archaeological Museum in Athens.
ⓐ Petros M. Nomikos Conference Centre, Firostefani
☎ 22860 23016 🕐 10.00–20.00 daily ❶ Admission charge

### Folklore Museum
Interesting collection of household utensils, farm tools, weapons, island costumes, weaving and spinning equipment.
ⓐ Kontohori ☎ 22860 22792

### Megaro Gyzi
An old residence that is now home to engravings from the last three centuries, paintings of Greek artists who worked on Santorini. The collection of old photographs gives a good idea of what Thira looked like before the 1956 earthquake.
ⓐ Erithrou Stavrou ☎ 22860 23077 🌐 www.megarogyzi.gr
🕐 10.00–16.00 Mon–Sat (May–Oct), closed Sun, closed Nov–Apr
❶ Admission charge

**COOKING THE SANTORINI WAY**
Learn how to cook and prepare *fava* with tomato caper sauce, aubergine salad with *taramasalata*, lamb in grapevine leaves, and cheese and honey pastry at the Selene Restaurant Cooking Class. Sessions include an introduction to Santorini wines, with four tastings accompanied by cheeses and sausages from nearby islands. Eat the fruits of your labour to conclude the course, enhanced by a bottle of Santorini wine. Book as far in advance as possible. ⓐ Selene Restaurant, Agiou Mina ⓣ 22860 22249 ⓦ www.selene.gr ⓛ 10.30–14.00 daily

### Museum of Prehistoric Thira
This museum is worth visiting chiefly for the finds from Akrotiri that are on display: wall paintings, pottery, seals and domestic items. The prize exhibit is a fine gold ibex figurine and also on show are fossils of plants that grew on the island long before humans arrived.
ⓐ Mitropoleos ⓣ 22860 23217 ⓦ www.culture.gr ⓛ 08.30–20.00 Tues–Sun, closed Mon ⓘ Admission charge

## TAKING A BREAK

### Bars & cafés
**Art Café** £ ❶ It is tempting to keep this quiet and elegant courtyard café a secret because it is a lovely spot and the space is not enormous. Restful views out to sea make it just the place for a mid-morning coffee, a Greek salad or a glass of wine. The café's name is justified by the display of the proprietor's paintings and sculptures inside the café. ⓐ Cori Rigas Apartments, Agiou Mina ⓣ 22860 25251 ⓦ www.coririgas.com ⓛ 08.00–23.00 daily

**Café del Mar £** ❷  White comfy chairs, primrose yellow parasols, stunning views of the caldera, a choice of styles of coffee, sticky sweets, ice creams and cocktails. ⓐ Gold Street ❶ 22860 21139 🕒 07.30–24.00 daily

**Café NRG £** ❸  Friendly, small eatery with a few stools and takeaway service of crêpes, tortillas and a range of coffees. Useful for taking a break in the early hours of the morning if partying in the nearby clubs and pubs. ⓐ Erithrou Stavrou ❶ 22860 24997 🕒 10.00–04.00 daily

**Lava Internet Café £** ❹  As well as the internet facility, the tables outside are just fine for a lazy drink and a snack. Crêpes, yogurts, salads and ice creams make up the menu. ⓐ Erithrou Stavrou ❶ 22860 25291 🕒 09.00–24.00 daily

**Franco's ££** ❺  The doyen of Thira's caldera-view cocktail bar-cafés offers Singapore Slings, the original Maria Callas champagne cocktail, all on colourful balconies with wonderful views. ❶ 22860 24428 ⓦ www.francos.gr 🕒 09.00–24.00 daily

**Restaurants**
**Cesare £** ❻  Close to the Archaeological Museum, Cesare lacks those stunning views of the caldera, but the set meals, like fish and salad with a beer or glass of wine, or the moussaka choice, are fine if you want an affordable meal. ⓐ Ipapadis ❶ 22860 24161 ⓦ www.cesarerestaurant-santorini.gr 🕒 12.00–22.00 daily

**Stani ££** ❼  Make your way to the very top of this restaurant for that special view. The menu is an appealing one and vegetarians could easily manage here as well. ⓐ Ipapadis ❶ 22860 23078 ⓦ www.stani.gr 🕒 12.00–23.00 daily

**Zafora** ££ ❽   This place has fabulous views of the seascape. Seafood is a little pricey, but you are paying for the location and there are some appealing drinks, like an Indian fig cocktail. Best to reserve a table in advance. ⓐ By the cable car entrance ❶ 22860 23203 ⓦ www.zafora-restaurant.gr ❶ 09.00–23.00 daily

## AFTER DARK

### Restaurants

**Koukoumavlos** £££   ❾   Generally regarded as one of the best restaurants on Santorini; be sure to make a reservation to enjoy the creative Mediterranean-style cuisine. The owner is the chef and Greeks come here as much as overseas visitors. To find Koukoumavlos, seek out the pathway at the side of the Atlantis hotel and it is only 100 m (328 ft) away. ⓐ Walkway between the cathedral and Agiou Mina ❶ 22860 23807 ⓦ www.koukoumavlos.eu ⓔ info@koukoumavlos.eu ❶ 19.30–24.00 daily

**Selene** £££ ❿   Selene is undoubtedly one of the finest restaurants on the island. Reserve a table here and enjoy food that uses the island's caper leaves, white aubergines and tiny tomatoes packed with flavour. Impressive, all-Greek wine list and first-class service. ⓐ Agiou Mina ❶ 22860 22249 ⓦ www.selene.gr ❶ 19.30–22.30 daily

### Bars & clubs

**Enigma** ⓫   Long before midnight there is a queue snaking its way down the narrow cobbled street to gain admission to what seems to be a small club; once inside, the size will surprise. ⓐ Erithrou Stavrou ❶ 22860 22123/22860 22466 ⓦ www.enigmaclub.gr ❶ 21.00–03.00 daily ❶ Cover charge includes first drink

Kira Thira Jazz Bar, Thira

**Kira Thira Jazz Bar** ⑫ The jazz music is not live, but the ambience is just right for a place calling itself by this name: small, with trumpets and an old saxophone hanging on the wall, it does a neat line in cocktails and spirits. ⓐ Erithrou Stavrou ❶ 22860 22770 ⏱ 18.00–04.00 daily

**Koo Club** ⑬ With five bars and a huge yard, this nightclub is as popular as Enigma and it always attracts a good crowd of revellers, especially at weekends. ⓐ Erithrou Stavrou ❶ 22860 22025 ⏱ 21.00–03.00 daily ❶ Cover charge includes first drink

**Murphy's** ⑭ Helped by the proximity of Thira's two best nightclubs, it is enormously popular and can get packed to the door at weekends. ⓐ Erithrou Stavrou ❶ 22860 22248 ⏱ 11.00–04.00 daily

**Porto Carra** ⑮ This pretty little café-bar, part of the hotel discreetly situated below it, is inviting at any time of the day or night, but a visit around sunset suggests itself because there are superb views across the caldera and watching the sun go down with an Irish coffee or cocktail or glass of champagne – or just a plain beer or a milkshake – might be the perfect end to a perfect day. ⓐ Agiou Mina ❶ 22860 22979 ⓦ www.hotelportocarra.com ⏱ 08.30–24.00 daily

▶ *Pirgos village*

# EXCURSIONS
Out & about

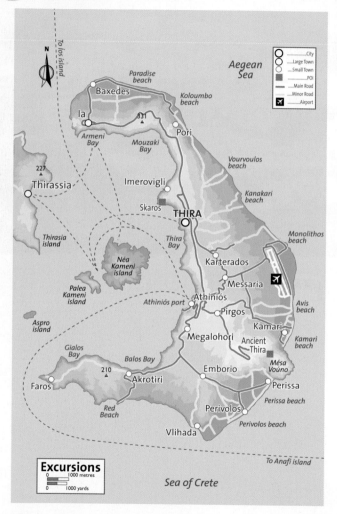

# Beach trips

### RED BEACH

Tucked away in the southwest of the island, Red Beach (Kókkini Ámmos) is distinguished by the massive slabs of red and black volcanic rock that tower behind it. The dark sand gets scorchingly hot so be sure to bring appropriate footwear. There are nearby restaurants and a drinks stall or two at the back of the beach but bring plenty of water and your own towels. In summer, Red Beach is a favourite excursion and because the area is small and enclosed the sandy beach soon becomes full of sunbathers. The clear water is excellent for snorkelling.

There are ten buses a day from Thira, starting at 08.45 (check the return times), to Akrotiri and it is a short walk from the bus terminal. If driving, there is a car park a couple of minutes' walk away from the beach. Boat trips to and from Red Beach are also

### BOAT TRIPS

Without your own transport, the most convenient way to undertake excursions is by way of the various tours that a number of different companies offer. Boat trips across the caldera are highly recommended because it is only when you are out there, floating above the submerged volcano, that the full majesty and uniqueness of Santorini make themselves felt. Some of the boat trips focus on the islands of Palea Kameni and Néa Kameni; others structure themselves around the more isolated beaches that are best reached from the sea. There are also bus trips that cover inland villages. Every resort has its quota of tour agents, but for details of the choices available check out the websites of major operators like Kamari Tours (Ⓦ www.kamaritours.com).

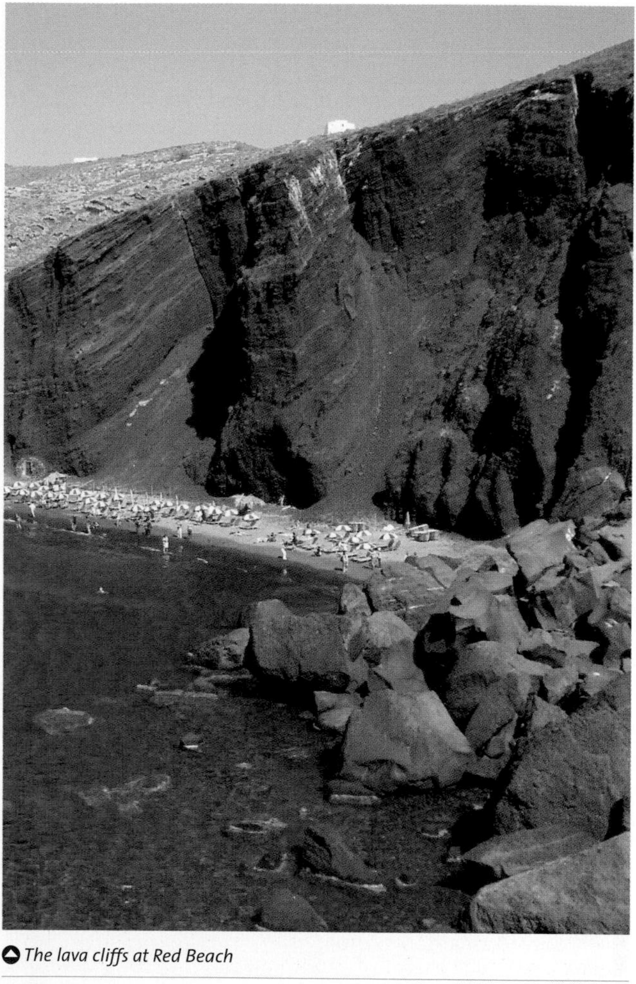

The lava cliffs at Red Beach

available from the main resort beaches and many of the island tours also include a visit.

A combined visit to the beach and the ancient site of Akrotiri could take a full day. As well as the two restaurants listed below, there are more in the nearby ancient village of Akrotiri (see page 71).

## TAKING A BREAK

### Restaurants & bars

**Glaros £** Fresh fish, fried tomato balls, *meze* served with paprika and home-made wine make up the appealing menu of this pleasant taverna. ⊜ On the way to Red Beach, a short way before Ta Delfinia ⊕ 22860 81168 ⊕ 08.00–23.30 daily

**Ta Delfinia £–££** This is the closest restaurant to Red Beach, a few minutes away on foot, and from the entrance there are steps down to tables idyllically positioned by the water's edge. Appetising starters – like *fava* or tomato balls, lots of fish dishes, including lobster spaghetti – and a wine list. Prices are reasonable, the food is good and the location superb. Ta Delfinia also has some rooms for rent. ⊜ Close to the beach ⊕ 22860 81151 ⊕ 08.30–23.00 daily

## MONOLITHOS

On the east coast of Santorini, Monolithos is an attractive beach with the same dark sands as elsewhere on the island. The water deepens here very gradually and in this respect it is the best beach for children; there is also a playground. For adults, Monolithos offers a quiet beach location where one can escape the hubbub of Kamari and Perissa. There are no bus services and you will need your own transport, but it is easy to reach by following signs to the airport. Instead of turning right into the airport, continue past it and you will see signs clearly pointing

○ *Dramatic cliffs on Monolithos beach*

the way to the beach. It is only a few minutes by car from the airport entrance.

## TAKING A BREAK

### Restaurants
**Saltsa £££** Midway between Thira and the cliffside suburb of Firostefani, Saltsa is noted for its modern approach to traditional Greek recipes, using fresh island produce and with a very good list of local wines. Not cheap, but a good place for a special occasion. ⓐ Firostefani ⓣ 22860 28018 ⓦ www.saltsa.gr ⓛ 19.00–23.00, Tues & Thur–Sun, closed Mon & Wed

# Island trips

### THIRASSIA

Now the second-largest island of the mini-archipelago, Thirassia was a part of Santorini until an eruption in 236 BC sheared it off from the mainland. There are different ways to experience Thirassia, either as part of a tour that takes in the island or by yourself, by hopping on one of the ferries that depart from Amoudi at Ia or from Athiniós port. The tour boats usually arrive at Kórfos, where there are a couple of tavernas and from where a pathway makes its way up to Manolas, 200 m (656 ft) above sea level.

△ *Rocky Palea Kameni*

## THINGS TO SEE & DO

There are no sandy beaches on Thirassia, so, with accommodation limited to a few rooms in Manolas and no nightlife, most people confine their visit to a few hours or half a day. On the plus side, there are tremendous views of the caldera on the journey to Thirassia and, once there, you can walk from Kórfos to Manolas and continue from there southwards by following an unpaved road. The further you walk southwards, the more you will have the island to yourself, and the seascape is a constant thrill to behold.

## TAKING A BREAK

### Restaurants & bars

Thirassia has only three or four transient tavernas and cafés, all of which are dedicated to servicing as many excursionists as possible in the shortest possible time and all of which fill up quickly as soon as the first day-trip boats arrive from Athiniós port and from the giant cruise ships which anchor in the caldera. There is little point in recommending any particular establishment – your best bet is to grab the first available chairs you see, as there is little to do on Thirassia except to enjoy the view from a café table.

## PALEA KAMENI & NÉA KAMENI

Referred to in the local tour literature as the 'burnt islands', this proves to be no exaggeration – especially when you see the charred and rocky Palea Kameni and Néa Kameni. Both are volcanically active, but safe to visit. Palea Kameni, with its offshore hot spring, is the older of the two, having come into existence in AD 157 as the result of an eruption. It was not until the early 18th century that Néa Kameni appeared on the scene.

## THINGS TO SEE & DO

Both islands are uninhabited and therefore have no restaurants or bars, but what you do get is the experience of walking on the relatively recent remains of a volcanic eruption and the opportunity to smother yourself in sulphurous mud – said to be therapeutic – and swim in hot springs. The standard morning trip, which every tour shop in your resort will offer, usually departs around 09.00 every day of the week. It starts with a journey by a tour bus to Athiniós port, from where you board the boat that sets off on a slow cruise across the caldera. Néa Kameni is often the first stop, with time for a walk up the volcano, followed by a longer stay on coal-coloured Palea Kameni in order to have time for a swim in the hot springs and a bath in the mud. You should be back in your resort in time for a late lunch.

❶ If visiting Néa Kameni and/or Palea Kameni, it is best not to wear light sandals or flip-flops because the ground is rocky and sharp. Also remember to bring your own supply of water.

# Inland trips

## MEGALOHORI

A peaceful village in a rural setting and one that most visitors are inclined to just pass through on their way from Thira, only 9 km (5½ miles) away, to the beaches or Akrotiri. It suggests itself, however, as a place to visit and not just for the nearby wineries. The cobbled streets do not lead to any particular places of interest but allow serendipity to prevail and encourage you to just take in the non-touristy side to Santorini.

## THINGS TO SEE & DO

### Boutari Winery

A modern winery that offers organised tours of the cellars and production facilities plus a multimedia presentation on the history of Santorini wines. As well as its standard annual production of mainly white wines, it also experiments with one new type each year, which can be tasted along with the others.

ⓐ Megalohori, signposted on the road to Akrotiri ❶ 22860 81011 ❶ 11.00–16.00 Mon–Fri, closed Sat & Sun ❶ Admission charge

### Gavala Vineyard

An interesting winery, though not one of the most visited, which produces two whites, one red and one sweet. There is also a small museum in a stone tunnel.

ⓐ Megalohori, signposted from the village square ❶ 22860 82552 ❶ 10.00–20.00 daily

## PIRGOS

The village of Pirgos, the oldest surviving settlement on the island, was once the capital of Santorini. The highlight of a visit here, apart from the intrinsic pleasure of leaving the beach

scene and experiencing inland life, is a walk up the stepped pathway to the remains of a Venetian fortress (*Pirgos* is Greek for 'tower'), where some old churches still stand. Along the way and at the top there are exhilarating views of the vineyard-covered countryside and the Aegean Sea in the distance. Both in the village itself and on the way to the summit, there are cafés at which you can enjoy a drink or meal. There are also a couple of attractive, small arts and crafts shops along the route to the summit. Only 3 km (2 miles) from the village, the **Profitis Ilías Monastery** (dating back to 1712) is situated on a mountain peak at an altitude of 566 m (1,857 ft). This is the highest point on the island and there are sweeping views, though the summit itself is spoilt by an amalgam of antennae and fencing belonging to a NATO listening station.

## THINGS TO SEE & DO

### Argyros Estate

The village of **Mésa Gonia**, where this winery is located, is just a few miles east of Pirgos and while it does not stay open for visitors on a daily basis, you are welcome to phone and arrange a tour of the facilities and taste some of the fine wines that are produced here. Nine types of wine are bottled: mostly white but also a lovely rosé, one red and two sweet wines.

ⓐ Mésa Gonia ⓣ 22860 31489 ⓦ www.estate-argyros.com
ⓛ By appointment only

### Hatzidakis Winery

This modest little winery, only in business for the last ten years, doesn't go out of its way to advertise itself but the four whites, one red and one sweet wine that it produces are rather special. It is well worth the trouble of phoning to arrange a visit, in order to experience the cave-like setting where the tanks are stored and taste the produce.

◯ *Pirgos village perched on its hill*

ⓐ Outside Pirgos, on your left on the road to the Profítis Ilías
Monastery ⓣ 22860 32552 ⓦ www.hatzidakiswines.gr
ⓔ hatzidakis@hatzidakiswines.gr ⓛ Apr–Oct, but phone to
arrange the time of your visit, closed Nov–Mar

### Icons & Relics Collection of Pirgos

Housed in a former Catholic church which stood abandoned
until the 1970s, this museum houses some superb 15th- and
16th-century icons, skilfully carved wooden crosses, and
gorgeous religious vestments.
ⓐ Agia Triada, Pirgos ⓣ 22860 31812 ⓛ 10.00–16.00 daily
ⓘ Admission charge

## TAKING A BREAK

### Restaurants & bars

**Franco's Café £** At the very top of the stepped walkway, Franco's
is ideal during the day for a coffee and a *meze* platter – large or
small – or *crostini* (toasted bread) with a topping of your choice.
If you come here to watch the sun going down, there are drinks
and cocktails – this is the only place on the island that regularly
serves up a Singapore Sling. The roof garden setting is very
attractive and there are grand views across the island. ⓐ Pirgos
Castelli ⓣ 22860 33957 ⓦ www.francos.gr ⓛ 10.00–22.00
Mon–Thur, 10.00–24.00 Fri & Sat, closed Sun

**Pyrgos Taverna £–££** Although sometimes monopolised by coach
parties, this is the most urbane of the eating options in Pirgos,
and there are some outdoor tables overlooking the surrounding
countryside. ⓐ On the road coming into the village from Thira
ⓣ 22860 31346 ⓦ www.pyrgos-santorini.com ⓛ 12.00–02.00 daily

**Kallisti ££** Kallisti is the best restaurant in Pirgos, serving
sophisticated versions of traditional Santorinian dishes, such as

aubergine dip made with the island's own white aubergines, and an array of other choices that emphasise fresh locally grown fruit and vegetables, lamb, chicken and seafood. There is also a good choice of the island's own wines. ⓐ Pirgos village centre ⓣ 22860 34108 ⓛ 12.00–15.00, 19.00–23.00 daily

## ANCIENT AKROTIRI

In the south of the island, the village of Akrotiri would be just a small village to pass through on the road to Red Beach, were it not for pieces of an ancient wall that kept appearing in the rubble when a nearby area was being cleared for the digging of pumice stone in the 1860s. The volcanic soil in the south of Santorini was used by the French engineer Ferdinand de Lesseps as insulation for the Suez Canal (built 1859–69) and it was during the process of excavating the land that artefacts accidentally came to the surface. This led to the first team of archaeologists coming to the island from France in 1870, but a century passed before the city of Akrotiri was discovered by the Greek archaeologist Spiros Marinatos. Under his supervision and direction, tunnels were made through the volcanic soil and what came to light were the extensive remains of a Minoan city that was destroyed by the volcanic eruption of 1600 BC. Before that catastrophe, Akrotiri was an important urban centre, trading with Crete, Cyprus, Egypt and Syria as well as the Greek mainland.

### A Minoan city

It was Marinatos who established the importance of Akrotiri as the largest and most significant colony of the Minoans on Crete. Trading links brought wealth to Strongili and evidence of this was brought to light when the richly decorated walls of houses in Akrotiri were unearthed in the 1960s. Every house in the city had at least one painted wall, the artwork presumably commissioned by the wealthy seamen and merchants who owned the houses.

🔺 *Mural of children boxing, Akrotiri*

## The eruption

As with Pompeii near Naples, Italy, the city of Akrotiri was completely buried by the eruption, and excavation work has revealed many aspects of ordinary life in a city now over 3,500 years old. Unlike Pompeii, the residents of Akrotiri had due warning of the impending disaster – presumably the volcano was violently active before it blew apart the island – and everyone was able to escape. They left behind their homes, two and even three storeys high, with rooms enlivened by colourful frescoes and items of domestic furniture that they couldn't carry away. Visitors can walk through the city, along the same footpaths that the original inhabitants used, and see – intact – the giant pots they used for storing wine and olive oil.

## Resurrecting Akrotiri

Excavating Akrotiri proved perilous and Spiros Marinatos was himself killed after a fall on the site – faithful to his request, his grave lies on one of the houses he excavated. Making the city safe and accessible for visitors, while preserving its architectural integrity, has proved to be a major reason for the current renovation work that is in progress. A sophisticated air treatment plant is being installed so as to minimise the build-up of carbon dioxide, exhaled by visitors, and a large-scale overhead shelter is being erected so that the site is protected from the elements. ⓦ www.culture.gr ⓛ Presently closed for renovation and restoration work; when reopened, likely to be closed on Mondays

## TAKING A BREAK

### Restaurants & bars

**Theofanis** £ On your right if coming into the village along the main road from Megalohori, this friendly taverna is fine for a late breakfast, a mid-morning break of iced coffee, or a full

meal. Spaghetti, veal, grills and fish make up the bulk of the menu, but there are interesting appetisers like Santorini's mashed split peas. ⓐ Akrotiri village ⓣ 22860 81141 ⓛ 09.00–22.30 daily

**Kapetan Dimitris £–££** Traditional taverna next to Akrotiri's famous lighthouse, with a great view from the veranda and a menu that emphasises meaty grills and hearty oven-cooked dishes. ⓐ Faros, Akrotiri ⓣ 22860 82210 ⓛ 12.00–22.00 daily

**Panorama £–££** As well as traditional Greek food like moussaka, stewed meatballs and all those delicious *meze* – try the ones using *saganaki* cheese – there are astonishing views across the bay to the towering cliffs. If you have your own transport, consider making an evening reservation and then dine by one of the window tables. Less expensive than the restaurants with similar views in Thira and Ia. ⓐ Before Akrotiri village, on the main road ⓣ 22860 81183 ⓛ 09.00–23.00 daily

## ANCIENT THIRA

Mésa Voúno, the hill that became home to Greek colonists in the 8th century BC, survived the eruption of 1600 BC because of its situation on the east coast, furthest from the volcano on the west side of the island. Occupying the stone terraces atop Mésa Voúno, the rocky headland separating Kamari from Perissa, are the remains of ancient Thira. Excavations began here in the 1890s and quickly revealed evidence of a settlement dating back to the 9th century BC. The city was inhabited for a millennium, its hilltop location (369 m/1,211 ft above sea level) always providing security and a clear line of sight to any hostile ships approaching from the sea. The city's main street runs in a north/northwest–southeast direction and under the Romans a sewerage system was laid down.

One of the chief attractions of the site is the small but perfectly formed theatre that looks down, dramatically one might say, to the sea. It requires a bit more imagination to conjure up scenes from the scanty remains of the temples and the agora (market area) that have been carefully unearthed by archaeologists. The acropolis was the natural location for colonists, thought to be from Sparta in mainland Greece, who came here to establish a city. They built roads down to Kamari and Perissa, the beaches where they probably first landed. The city was developed extensively during the Hellenistic period, beginning in the early 4th century BC, and it remained an important settlement in Roman times. It was not until the 3rd century AD that the city began to decline in importance.

Ancient Thira can be reached by a very short journey with your own transport from Kamari or Perissa and it can also be walked from either resort. The best way to reach the site on foot is by way of the uphill path from Perissa (see page 41).
🕐 08.30–15.00 Tues–Sun, closed Mon

> The only place to find food or drink near ancient Thira is from a mobile van that occasionally parks at the top of the road, so consider bringing food for a picnic; at the very least, bring plenty of water.

## THINGS TO SEE & DO

Though founded in the 9th century BC, most of what you see today dates back to the time of the Ptolemies (300–150 BC), when Thira served as the garrison for an important Egyptian naval station patrolling this region of the Aegean. Your first ancient site, however, is later still – a chapel from the Byzantine era that stands close to the main entrance. As you walk past this you stroll along what were once walkways through the Egyptian

garrison town, and there is a sign indicating the site of the agora (market area). Remains include the base of a temple dedicated to Dionysus, assorted houses and the theatre (at the time of writing this is closed for restoration work). Much of what you see is not clearly identified for visitors and the educational value of a visit is much diminished because of this. There are, however, plans underway to improve this situation.

◔ Ruins in ancient Thira

# Trips to neighbouring islands

## Íos

> There are regular ferries between Santorini and Íos
> (which has no airport) and fast daily Super Jet services that
> take only an hour. Tickets can be booked online at
> ⓦ www.seajets.gr or make enquiries with one of the tour
> agents in your resort.

Íos does not aspire to the sophistication of Santorini, but for
young people seeking a party atmosphere this little island is
hard to beat. You will arrive at Gialos (Yialos) and there is a
good beach within walking distance; if time is short then you
might want to take up one of the offers of accommodation in
Gialos, which will be proffered as you step off the boat. There is
also a useful accommodation booking office at the port, should
you wish to consider options before making a decision about
where to stay. Hora (also called Íos Town) is the main town, a
short bus journey or a 20-minute walk away, and here you
will find lots of accommodation. Hora is also the centre of
the island's nightlife and there are any number of bars and
clubs that stay open until 03.00 every morning of the week
during summer.

### THINGS TO SEE & DO

#### Manganari beach
If Milopotas (see page 79) is just a bit too full-on, then
Manganari, on the south coast, might be the antidote. It is easy
to reach by the daily boat taxi from Gialos, which departs each
morning and there is also a bus service. Accommodation here is
more expensive and the nightlife is serene when compared to
Milopotas, but during the day this is the place to lay back and

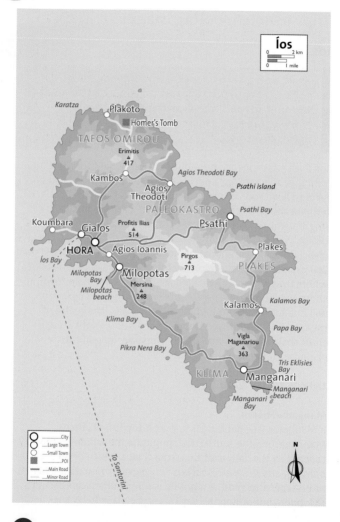

Íos

0    2 km
0    1 mile

Karatza

Plakoto

Homer's Tomb

TAFOS OMIROU

Erimitis
▲
417

Kambos

Agios Theodoti Bay

Agios
Theodoti

Psathi island

PALEOKASTRO

Psathi Bay

Koumbara

Gialos

Profitis Ilias
▲
514

Psathi

HORA

Agios Ioannis

Plakes

Íos Bay

Pirgos
▲
713

PLAKES

Milopotas Bay

Milopotas

Milopotas beach

Mersina
▲
248

Klima Bay

Kalamos Bay

Kalamos

Papa Bay

Pikra Nera Bay

Vigla
Maganariou
▲
363

Tris Eklisies
Bay

KLIMA

Manganari

Manganari
beach

Manganari
Bay

○ ......City
◎ ......Large Town
○ ......Small Town
■ ......POI
━ ......Main Road
— ......Minor Road

N

To Santorini

acquire that bronze tan. Though officially discouraged, nude sunbathing is still acceptable here.

### Milopotas beach

This is easily the best beach on the island, not just due to its beautiful stretch of sand but also because it is particularly well organised for watersports (see below). It is also easy to reach by bus. There are plenty of places to stay, lots of bars and restaurants and late-night beach parties are not exactly unheard of here.

### Watersports

There are other outfits offering some of the same but this company, Meltemi Extreme Watersports, has gained a good reputation. For absolute beginners, lessons are available in waterskiing and windsurfing, and for pure fun there are canoes, tubes and banana boats. Snorkelling equipment can also be rented.

ⓐ Milopotas beach ⓣ 22860 91680
ⓦ www.meltemiwatersports.com

## TAKING A BREAK

### Restaurants & bars

**Lord Byron £–££** This taverna succeeds, against the odds, at creating a traditional Greek atmosphere and Greek cuisine in a heady and hedonistic island. Come here for an alternative to the usual menu – the *meze* alone will satisfy vegetarians – and the wines from Santorini are a bonus. ⓐ Hora ⓣ 22860 92125
ⓛ 08.30–23.30 daily

**Drakos ££** Excellent fish taverna with a fine range of imaginative seafood dishes such as stuffed squid, octopus in fennel and orange sauce, and shrimp and mussel *giouvetsi* (casserole with pasta). ⓐ Milopotas ⓣ 22860 91281 ⓦ www.drakostaverna.gr
ⓛ 11.00–23.00 daily

**Elpis ££** Try the superb *kakavia* (fish stew) at this traditional seafood taverna overlooking the little harbour at Milopotas or sample a range of other seafood and oven-cooked dishes.
ⓐ Milopotas ☎ 22860 91626 🕐 11.00–23.00 daily

**To Katoi ££** This excellent *mezedopoleion* (*meze* restaurant) is a great place for a glass of *ouzo*, wine or beer with an array of nibbles, but you can equally happily spend a whole evening here, ordering *meze* after *meze* as the mood takes you.
ⓐ Hora ☎ 22860 91179 🕐 11.00–24.00 daily

### Clubs
### Kandi
Smaller, more intimate but still very lively lounge and dance club with space to chill inside and outside. A bit less raunchy than some of its competitors. ⓐ Main street, Hora 🕐 22.00–03.00 daily

### Planet Ios
Biggest and wildest of the island's clubs, with three bars, a VIP section and room for 1,000 people. Reopened under new management in summer 2009 but keeps up its policy of bringing in world-class DJs and hosting over-the-top evenings.
ⓐ Main street, Hora 🕐 22.00–03.00 daily

### ANAFI
Served by regular ferries from Santorini that reach Anafi in an hour and a half (check ⓦ www.gtp.gr), this is a tiny island retreat for people who want both the beauty of Santorini, without the crowds, and the beaches of Íos, without in-your-face hedonism. There are few buses and no taxis on this island and, unless you hire a motorbike, it is possible to get around relying on foot power. There is a single village on the island, Hora, characterised by blindingly white-coloured buildings that could be mistaken for snow when you look at the photographs

you have taken. The accommodation is limited and in high season it would be advisable to have somewhere booked in advance. There are some very nice places to stay in comfort, with prices that compare very favourably with those of Santorini. Check out, for example, Ta Plagia (☎ 22860 61372 ⓦ www.taplagia.gr), which offers bed and breakfast, or the more classy Villa Apollon (☎ 22860 61348 ⓦ www.apollonvillage.gr), which has air-conditioned rooms and an idyllic garden setting. Visit ⓦ www.taplagia.gr or make an arrangement through a tour agency on Santorini.

## THINGS TO SEE & DO

### Beaches

You can walk to **Klisidi**, east of the port where ferries arrive, which is a very small beach but perfectly formed and ideal for swimming and paddling. The prize beach is **Roukounas**, stretching unblemished for 500 m (1,640 ft) and with plenty of shade during the heat of the day.

🔺 *Strikingly white buildings in Anafi*

### Monastery of Zoodohos Pigi

The monastery is not open to the public but the two-hour walk (or you can also catch a bus for most of the way) is a highlight of any stay on the island. Along the way you pass a ruined temple to Apollo and, always, there are breathtaking views of the Aegean and the surrounding countryside. There are no cafés in the area so bring sufficient water and some snacks. If you are here in early September, the monastery opens its doors and a local festival is celebrated with dance and merriment.
ⓐ Katalimatsa ⓣ 22860 99965

## TAKING A BREAK

### Restaurants & bars

**Margarita Restaurant £–££** Open for breakfast, lunch and dinner, serving home-made pizzas and sweets, fresh fish, grills and *meze*, and other home-cooked dishes. ⓣ 22860 61237 ⓛ 09.00–22.00 daily

**Mantres Bar ££** Lively and colourful bar with a good choice of drinks, snacks and music (occasionally live). ⓐ Klisidi ⓣ 22860 61237 ⓛ 19.00–24.00 daily

▶ *Village balcony on a lane in Pirgos*

# LIFESTYLE
Island life

# Food & drink

Greek cuisine traditionally relies on fresh ingredients and lots of olive oil, with an emphasis on fish and delicious appetisers. The best places to eat on Santorini reflect this heritage and the Mediterranean approach to food still dominates, but what justifies the notion of a Santorini mini-cuisine, or at the very least gives an individuality to some of the dishes waiting to be enjoyed there, is the availability and use of local vegetables that are cultivated on the island's volcanic soil – and with remarkably little watering. Add to this the Santorini wines and you have some food and drink experiences that are not typical of other Greek islands.

Breakfast tends to be a light affair, rarely available before 08.00, and most hotels, even when there is a self-serving buffet system, do not cater for the 'full English/American breakfast' as a matter of course. There will be plenty of fresh bread, usually more than one variety of loaf, and often including brown bread, buns and rolls as well as croissants. Cold ham, cheese, olives, tomatoes and cucumber make up the usual array of offerings, but you can also expect eggs to be available, often in the form of omelettes, though scrambled and hard-boiled eggs are not uncommon.

Lunch is not the main meal of the day for most Greeks and is often eaten in the early afternoon, but in the resorts all the places to eat are up and running by 12.00. Dinner comes late, often 22.00, but most restaurants on Santorini are ready to serve dinner from early evenings onwards. Only the more sophisticated restaurants have a set opening time for evening meals, usually 19.00 or 19.30.

Desserts are not always the best part of traditional Greek cuisine, especially if you are looking forward to rich chocolate concoctions. Sweet cakes with cream or syrup are more characteristic, but the ice creams are often a treat, especially if they are home-made.

🔺 *Dining in Thira*

A meal usually begins with bread brought to your table – often charged for so check it is fresh – and this is best enjoyed with whatever dips you order from the *meze* (hors d'oeuvres) section of the menu. Some appetisers, like *tzatziki* and *saganaki* (see page 92), appear on most menus but most restaurants will have their own favourites and, because menus are always in English, it is easy to know in advance what you are ordering. Menus often have sections devoted to pizzas, pasta, fish, meat and desserts. Carnivores should not expect to find large steaks on a menu as the preference is for grilled meats like young lamb, veal or chicken. Portions are usually small when compared to English or American expectations. If you want your salad served before or with a main course, it is best to specify this when ordering.

Tavernas, the traditional Greek eating place, are more informal than a regular restaurant and if a place calls itself a taverna then you should expect reasonable prices and a fair selection of *meze* and main courses to choose from. In some of the resorts, Kamari and Perissa in particular, you will, if you are unlucky, experience a meal that is at best mediocre. They tend to be the ones that try a little too hard to entice you into their premises. In the best fish restaurants, the best fish and seafood is priced by weight. Choose your fish from the ice counter; it is then weighed and priced for your approval before being dispatched to the kitchen. By law, restaurants are required to indicate on the menu if fish or meat have been previously frozen.

Tipping is at your discretion and should depend on the quality of the service and the food. A service charge is not usually added to the bill.

**LOCAL FOOD**

Santorini has some specialities in food that should be tasted. The humble *fava* (yellow split pea) is grown on the island and used to make a tasty purée for an appetiser; it is also used as an

**SANTORINI'S CAPER LEAVES**

The caper grows wild on the island and the leaves are collected for their intense, almost spicy taste. They are used chiefly in salads and small bottles of the leaves can be purchased and brought home to add some zest to the next salad you prepare.

ingredient in main dishes. The island is also famous for its small tomatoes, cultivated but never watered, which are often turned into small balls, after mixing with onions and spearmint, ready for frying. White aubergines are another island product, used in casseroles and adding a sweet taste that is not the same as the more usual purple-coloured variety.

Santorini is also famous for its caper leaves and a good way to appreciate their taste is by looking out for a Santorini Salad on a restaurant menu. The more touristy kind of restaurant will not feature this but places like Selene in Thira (page 54), perhaps the restaurant most dedicated to using local produce, or Ta Dihtia in Perissa (page 45), serve up the classic version using the island's small tomatoes, cucumber, marinated anchovies, capers and caper leaves, and *chloro* cheese. On the dessert front, look for *melitinia* – a small cream cheese pie that is flavoured with *mastika*. Made from the gum of a tree grown on Chios, *mastika* has an unusual taste and can be used creatively in the kitchen.

Seafood is always available and Santorini is the place to enjoy octopus, squid and cuttlefish as well as the kind of fish, like bream and bass, which many holidaymakers will be more used to. Lobster is often listed on menus as a plate for two people to share.

## PICNIC FOOD

It is easy to make up a picnic, though it helps if your hotel room has a fridge where you can keep some of the ingredients.

## THE SANTORINI TOMATO

Originally from Egypt, the cherry tomato that is grown on Santorini has a particularly rich taste that is due to the island's unique ecosystem. Small in size, it has a hard skin and, because it is never watered (except by the humidity overnight), it packs a tasty punch because of the more-than-average amount of sugar inside.

The first place to find is the local bakery or, failing that, a mini-market with daily early-morning deliveries of bread and buns. Cans of olives are everywhere – the largish Kalamata ones are a treat – and look out also for yogurt in a suitable container. There are plenty of cheeses available as well as plums and other fruits to make up a delicious picnic lunch.

### DRINKS

The national alcoholic beverage is *ouzo*, a white spirit mixed with aniseed and fennel that gives it a highly characteristic taste. Usually served with ice and a glass of water, *ouzo* turns cloudy when the water is added. Despite its powerful taste and aroma, *ouzo* is no higher in alcohol than most other European spirits, and is in fact less potent than many brands of whisky, vodka and gin.

## WINE TASTING

All the wineries offer tasting sessions of their own products, but the Heliotopos Hotel in Imerovigli has a wine-tasting event each Tuesday night that brings together six wines from six different producers of wine on the island. The setting for this event – inside a cave – is unusual and adds to the oenological experience.

ⓐ Part of the hotel complex in Imerovigli ⓣ 22860 23670 ⓦ http://hotel.heliotopos.net

◔ *Try some wine at a wine tasting*

The Greek beer Mythos, a lager that is a little sweet, competes with the usual international brands that most bars stock on the island.

*Ouzo* can be found in supermarkets around the world, but Santorini wines are an island speciality, which depend on the volcanic soil for their unique taste. There are few springs on Santorini and the vines depend on the humidity at night for their water. They are also grown very close to the ground in order to protect them from the winds and in this respect a Santorini vineyard is an unusual sight. Look out for the *Nykteri* wine, a barrel-aged, slightly smoky dry white, the *Caldera*, which is a dry red wine, and the *Vinsanto*, which is a well-known sweet wine. There are three chief types of Santorini grapes – *asyrtiko*, *athiri* and *aidani* – but the one you are most likely to enjoy as a wine is the *asyrtiko*, characterised by high acidity. Named from the Greek word for 'night' (*nykta*), *Nykteri* wine was traditionally made at night and is now one of Santorini's most famous wines.

Greek coffee – thick, strong and served in tiny cups – is an acquired taste. It comes sweet (*glikou*), semi-sweet (*metriou*) or unsweetened (*skieto*) and is always accompanied by a glass of cold water.

Instant coffee – usually called *Nes* – is no longer the only alternative to the local brew; filter coffee, espresso and cappuccino are all widely available. Iced coffee (*frappe*) is simply made – just take one spoonful of instant coffee powder, add water and a handful of ice cubes, and blend.

*Meze* and *Easy Mediterranean* (both from Ryland Peters & Small) are two good cookbooks and, for everything about Greek cuisine, *The Food and Cooking of Greece* (Lorenz Books).

## VEGETARIANS

It is easy not to eat meat in Santorini's restaurants because there is always a great choice of appetisers and salads. By choosing a few *meze* and a salad, two people could enjoy a lunch together and the only drawback is that there is little alternative to this format. A more substantial meal could be created by adding to this a pizza or pasta dish, and it should not be difficult to find ones on the menu without any meat. Given that English is widely spoken, it is usually not difficult to explain that you are vegetarian (*hortofagos*) and some, though not many, restaurants do have vegetarian dishes listed on the menu. Look for *briam* (oven-baked vegetable casserole) and *dolmades* (stuffed vine leaves).

⬤ *Santorini salad makes a fresh and light lunch*

# Menu decoder

**APPETISERS/MEZE**

**Boureki** Vegetable and cheese pie

**Dolmades** Vine leaves stuffed with rice, herbs and a variety of fillings, which may be vegetarian or include meat

**Fassólia Saláta** White beans dressed with olive oil, lemon juice, parsley, onions, olives and tomatoes

**Loukanika** Small sausages

**Melizanosalata** Dip made from aubergines, tomatoes, onions and lemon juice

**Saganaki** Fried cheese appetiser

**Taramasalata** Smoked cod's roe dip made from puréed potatoes, oil and lemon juice

**Tiropitakia** Triangles of filo pastry stuffed with feta cheese and egg

**Tzatziki** Grated cucumber and garlic in a yogurt, olive oil and vinegar dressing

**FISH**

**Astakos** Lobster

**Bakaliaros** Greek salt cod

**Fangri** Bream

**Garides** Shrimp

**Kalamari** Squid

**Ksifias** Swordfish

**Lithrinia** Bass

**Soupies** Cuttlefish

**MAIN COURSES**

**Arni** Lamb

**Bifteki** Minced steak served as a hamburger without a bun

**Giouvetsi** Pasta casserole

**Hirino** Pork

**Keftedes** Meatballs

**Kleftiko** Baked lamb with garlic and vegetables

**Kotopoulo** Chicken

**Kouneli** Rabbit
**Moskari** Veal
**Moussaka** Layers of minced lamb and aubergine with béchamel sauce
**Pastitsio** Layers of macaroni, minced meat and haloumi cheese cooked with onions, tomatoes and basil topped with béchamel sauce
**Souvláki** Pork or lamb skewered and cooked over charcoal

**SALADS**
**Angouri** Cucumber
**Domates** Tomatoes
**Katsouni** A type of cucumber grown on Santorini
**Koukia** Mashed Fava beans

**VEGETABLES**
**Kremidi** Onions
**Pantsaria** Beetroot
**Patates** Potatoes
**Piperies** Peppers

**CHEESES**
**Feta** Cheese mostly made from sheep's milk but sometimes from goat's
**Haloumi** A hard cheese from Cyprus
**Kasseri** Hard cheese
**Myzethra** Whey cheese

**DESSERTS**
**Baklava** Nuts and honey in pastry
**Halva** Crushed sesame seeds and sugar
**Kourabiethes** Sugary biscuits
**Pagoto** Ice cream

**DRINKS**
**Bira** Beer
**Frappe** Iced coffee
**Gala** Milk
**Kafe** Coffee
**Karafa** Carafe
**Retsina** Resinated (infused with resin) wine
**Tsai** Tea

🔺 Art shop, Ia

# Shopping

OK, all the resorts have their quota of plaster-cast figurines of Zeus and his fellow Olympians, playing cards sets featuring naughty scenes from ancient Greek pottery, T-shirts galore, inexpensive costume jewellery, key rings, and bits and bobs, but, having said this, the level of mediocre merchandise here is remarkably modest.

Santorini is one of the most stylish and refined of all the Greek islands and you would expect the shopping scene to reflect this. You will not be disappointed. Thira has the best shopping possibilities, quantitatively and qualitatively, although Ia runs a close second in some respects and can outshine Thira in ethnic art. Both Thira and Ia have small boutiques selling fashionable designer clothes for women (for posh frocks, put plenty of time aside for some serious shopping). The standard of shopping falls noticeably in Kamari and Perissa, but both these resorts still have a number of shops where you could spend more money than you bargained for. All the better shops accept credit cards and prices tend to be fixed, although the art of gentle persuasion should result in a 10 per cent reduction from the marked price. It is not unknown for canny shoppers to obtain significantly higher discounts than this – though shops that lower their prices too easily are usually charging way over the top in the first place.

## SHOPPING IN THIRA

One of the main cobbled streets in Thira, Ipapadis (also spelt Ypapantis and Hypapantis), that runs between the Archaeological Museum and the Hotel Atlantis, is sometimes called Gold St because of the number of jewellery shops. As a general rule when it comes to shopping in Thira, if you have time, delay any intended purchase until you have had time to compare what you see with the shops in Ia. The largest shop on the island for clothes and footwear, for men and women, is Marios in the Ermis Shopping Centre in Thira.

❶ Some of the jewellery stores in Thira and Ia are too exclusive, focusing narrowly on cruise-ship customers and with prices that are no bargain. The shops that stock Greek-designed jewellery tend to be smaller in size and more affordable.

## SHOPPING IN IA

The number of shops in Ia is restricted simply by the small size of the place and the strict regulations when it comes to putting up new buildings. The shops that are to be found in the narrow and pedestrianised streets are uniformly of a high standard. Ia is especially appealing when it comes to shopping for arts-and-crafts items for the home, particularly paintings, pottery and small sculptures. Reproductions based on the frescoes from Akrotiri and from Knossos, the main centre of Minoan civilisation on Crete, are very eye-catching – though it helps when they are displayed outside a shop in the pure light of a Mediterranean summer; the likelihood is that they will not look quite so stunning when hanging on your wall back home.

❶ Handsome jewellery – silver more often than gold – that has been crafted in the workshops of Greek designers represents the best of what Santorini has to offer; in this area, Thira and Ia have the best shops.

## SHOPPING OUTSIDE THIRA & IA

The shops in both Kamari and Perissa tend to be off the main beach, occupying instead the small streets that run down to the beach. Aimed squarely at the holidaymaker, some of the best buys are beachwear, summer garments for women, sandals and bags. If you have your own transport, shopping is enhanced by the ability to stop off at individual places located by the side of main roads. In Megalohori, for example, the Akron Art Centre (ⓦ www.wallpaintings-greece.com) has sizeable premises displaying its stock of ancient art replicas: wall paintings, vases and mosaics. Worldwide delivery can be arranged here.

## BRINGING IT HOME

If you are coming from another EU country, there are no restrictions on what you can bring back or ship home. If you are minded to buy artwork that is too large to fit in your luggage then look for a shop that will pack and post it home for you. Rates are not exorbitant and if you pay by credit card you will have some redress if the goods never arrive, though retailers in Santorini do not go in for blatant rip-offs like this.

Given the current airline prohibitions on liquids in hand luggage, it is not possible to easily bring home a bottle or two of Santorini wine. Some wineries, like Art Space for example (see page 30), are dealing with this problem by packing their bottles securely so that they can be part of your checked-in luggage. There is a small tax-free shop at Santorini airport which offers a small selection of local wines which you can take on board your plane. What you can wrap securely for yourself are small bottles of Santorini's caper leaves and pack these into your checked-in luggage. Also, if your taste buds have experienced the pleasure of *mastika*-flavoured yogurt or ice cream and if you have some shopping time at Athens airport, there is a shop there devoted to the product (see page 112) and you can bring some home in a variety of forms.

# Children

The Greek attitude to holidaymakers with children is a very welcoming one and there are no problems when it comes to booking hotel rooms or bringing kids out to restaurants. A family dining out at night is a Greek pastime and children are invariably welcome and accommodated without a moment's notice. Many tavernas and restaurants will have highchairs with fitted trays for toddlers. Also, because so many places to eat have outdoor tables, the problem of young children playing around restaurant tables can be avoided by reserving a suitably placed table.

### ACTIVITIES

Kamari and Perissa are more suitable for families with children than the more urban and adult-oriented Thira and Ia. However, the beaches of pebbles and black sand are not toddler-friendly. They become painfully hot under the summer sun and are often windswept. Traffic on the main streets of both resorts, which separate most hotels from the beach, can be dangerous and younger children must not be left to cross roads unsupervised. If you are visiting Santorini with kids, choose accommodation with a pool. Several hotels in Kamari and Perissa have pools for toddlers and younger children as well as full-size pools. Older children (with parental supervision) can enjoy a wide range of watersports, including kayaking, windsurfing, rubber-ring and 'banana' rides and snorkelling. **Santorini Water Park** at Perissa, with its children's pools and water slides, is a sure-fire hit with children of all ages – the only snag is that they may want to come back here every day. Few of the island's other attractions and excursions are likely to appeal to younger visitors, but the boat trip to the crater of Palea Kameni (see page 65), where you are encouraged to wallow in volcanic mud, is one trip that they may enjoy; the

⬤ *Children might enjoy the open-air cinema in Kamari*

cable-car ride from Thira to the quayside at Skála (see page 49) is fun for older, bolder children.

## MEALTIMES

Feeding young children can be a challenge if they are not used to Mediterranean-style food. Exquisitely tasting dips, salads and seafood may not immediately convert your child into a young gourmet, and the tavernas of Kamari and Perissa are more resourceful than those of Thira and Ia when it comes to delivering a plate of chips and sausages with tomato sauce. In Kamari and Perissa, the majority of restaurants are on the beach and facing the sea and this is a great advantage because your children can run around to their hearts' content and yet remain within sight. In Thira and Ia this is not so easily arranged and because restaurants are squeezed into tight spaces, the boredom threshold for young children drops sharply.

# Sports & activities

Watersports are the big draw and the beach resorts of Kamari and Perissa are the places to base yourself in order to make the best of what's available.

### DIVING & SNORKELLING

The crystal-blue Aegean is ideal for snorkelling and diving. There are diving schools based in all the resorts and one of the better-known and long-established ones is the Volcano Diving Centre at Kamari ❶ 22860 33177 Ⓦ www.scubagreece.com. Experienced divers can rent equipment and may wish to enquire about the opportunities for wreck dives at 20–30 m (66–98 ft) in the open sea. Absolute beginners can embark on a new experience by way of a PADI training course with professional instructors.

A boat trip around the submerged crater, 10 km (6 miles) in diameter, is a favourite activity with many visitors, and one that you are not likely to forget because of the perspective it provides of the island's cliffs, the way Thira and Ia are perched on the edges and the awesome seascape that surrounds you. Every travel agency in every resort can arrange such trips and there are various options: traditional sailing boats, small ferries or glass-bottomed vessels. Standard tours depart between 09.00 and 10.30; sunset cruises with dinner on board usually depart at 17.00. Prices range from €15 for a straightforward trip to €40 for an evening cruise; small groups can also hire a private water taxi for the day and explore around the island. Easy Travel (❶ 22860 82880) have agents in all the resorts and Kamari Travel (❶ 22860 32750 Ⓦ www.kamaritours.com) is another well-established company with a range of boat trips, and so too is Pelican Travel (❶ 22860 22220 Ⓦ www.pelican.gr).

🔺 *Fun on the water at the Kamari Beach Centre*

## WALKING

Walking in the early morning or early evening is a pleasurable activity on Santorini because it is safe, the distances are not tremendous and no special equipment is required. Do, however, carry your own supply of water, and some form of headgear is useful in keeping the sun off the back of your neck. The walk from Perissa to ancient Thira (see page 41) is recommended: a return trip takes about two hours, it is impossible to get lost and there are great views to enjoy along the way. Other walks include the trip, up or down or both, between Thira and the small port below the town (see page 49) and a walk between Emborio and Vlihada that takes in some picturesque old windmills.

## WATERSPORTS

Beginners as well as the experienced can enjoy jet-skiing, kiteboarding, waterskiing and windsurfing, and instruction in the fun-filled art of wakeboarding and knee-boarding is also available. Learning programmes are based around half a day, a whole day or even a week. The **3sxsport+fun** at Kamari beach is a large operation and their courses and prices are worth checking out. ☎ 6932 780852 Ⓦ www.3sxsport.gr

LIFESTYLE

# Festivals & events

During summer there are various festivals taking place around the island, many of which have their cultural origins in grape harvesting. Each village also has a church festival celebrating its patron saint and these local events are characterised by a bazaar in the village square, with stalls offering local produce and home-made wine.

### FEBRUARY
**Ia:** Feast of Ipapandi on 2 February at Finikia, close to Ia.

### MAY
**Akrotiri:** Feast of Agios Epiphanios on 12 May.
**Thira:** Feast of Agios Theodosia in Thira takes place on 29 May.

### JULY
**Megalohori:** Feast of Agios Anargiri on 1 July.
**Monolithos:** Feast of Agios Ioannis on 24 July.

### AUGUST
**Ia:** Church festival, Feast of Agios Epta Paidion, on 4 August.
**Thira:** In mid-August, there is a two- to three-day event known as Ephesteia, with traditional dances and firework displays designed to remind everyone of the volcano. There is also a colourful recreation of a traditional Santorini wedding ceremony.
**Kamari:** A four-day Kamari Sea Feast starts in the middle of August and features music concerts on the beach and a traditional bazaar in the nearby village of Mésa Gonia. The festivities at Mésa Gonia are worth attending because this is the best-organised village festival on the island. The Feast of Panagia Mirtidiotissa is also celebrated at Kamari on 24 September each year.

**Pirgos:** There are nearly 50 churches in the vicinity of Pirgos, and the more important ones, including the monastery of Profítis Ilías, the church of Eisodion of Theotokou and the church of Koimisis of Theotokou, hold a procession on 14 August each year.

**Akrotiri:** Church festival on 15 August.

**Imerovigli:** Two churches in this village celebrate their patron saints on 29 August.

**Perissa:** Church festival, Feast of Agios Ioannis, on 29 August.

### SEPTEMBER

**Thira:** In early September for a fortnight there is a music festival at the Nomikos Conference Centre in Thira (☎ 28860 23166), featuring classical and jazz music; further information on this event is available at ⓦ www.santorini.info/music-festival.

🔺 *St John the Baptist church in Thira*

Most performances take place around 21.00 and tickets are about €25.

**Perissa:** Church festival, Feast of Agios Ioannis, is held on 14 September.

**Thirasia:** Feast of Panagia Giatrena on 21 September.

## OCTOBER

**Emborio:** Feast of Agios Averkios is held on 22 October. St Averkios, the patron saint of wine, is a kind of Christian Dionysus and copious amounts of wine are traditionally consumed on this day.

### GETTING MARRIED ON SANTORINI

Have your own festival by arranging your wedding and honeymoon on Santorini. You can be sure of fine weather, and sunset is the most popular time to hold the event. Both of you will need to show original copies of your birth certificates. A number of hotels organise the paperwork and make the necessary arrangements, and tour operators may offer various wedding packages. An internet search will help to find the hotels offering this service.

▶ *Getting about Santorini*

# PRACTICAL INFORMATION
Tips & advice

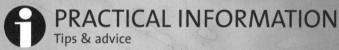

# Accommodation

This price guide is for a double room in high season including breakfast:

**£** = under €50   **££** = €50–€75   **£££** = over €75

### AKROTIRI
**Mathios Village ££–£££** You will not be in one of the resort areas but if this is not an issue then Mathios Village has a lot to offer.
ⓐ Akrotiri ① 22860 81152 ⓦ www.vmathios.gr

### IA
**Finikia's Place ££** Less than a 15-minute walk outside the centre of Ia, with a pool, sea view balconies and a good restaurant.
ⓐ Finikia, Ia ① 22860 71373 ① 22860 71118
ⓦ www.finikiaplace.com

**Fanari Villas ££–£££** The rooms are pleasantly decorated in a style fitting the cultural appeal of Ia, though you need to specify if you want a shower or a bath in the bathroom. The pool is a little special, half of it having a cave-like setting, plus there is a restaurant as well. ⓐ Ia ① 22860 71007 ⓦ www.fanarivillas.com

**Canaves Ia £££** Hotels do not come much more discreet than this: all the rooms and suites have their own verandas with views of the caldera, and can be reached without traipsing through a lobby. Top-class facilities, poolside restaurant – with breakfast served in your room or veranda – and professional service throughout. Children under 13 are not accommodated.
ⓐ Ia ① 22860 71453 ⓦ www.canaves.gr

**Golden Sunset Villas £££** Superb location on the tip of Santorini, where everyone passes by to watch the sunset. The villas are for two to four people; cots for babies also available. An old windmill has been restored and accommodates up to four. ⓐ Ia ☎ 22860 71001 ⓦ www.goldensunsetvillas.com

## KAMARI

**Irini's Rooms £** Virtually on the beach, air-conditioned rooms with fridge, a restaurant and café. ⓐ Kamari ☎ 22860 31246 ⓦ www.irinis-santorini.com

**The Boathouse Hotel ££** A pool, beach setting and rooms with sea views; under the same management as the friendly Almira restaurant (see page 34). ⓐ Kamari Beach ☎ 22860 33477 ⓦ www.boathousehotel.com

**Hotel Kastelli £££** The best place to stay in Kamari, off the beach but only a two-minute walk from the expanses of black sand. The double rooms, stylishly and colourfully decked out, have queen-sized beds. There is more than one pool, a poolside restaurant and a fitness area with a sauna and steam room. ⓐ Kamari ☎ 22860 31530 ⓦ www.kastelliresort.com

## MEGALOHORI

**Vedema Resort £££** Rather grand accommodation with all the facilities you would expect from an expensive hotel, including a spa, and a virtually private beach within walking distance. ⓐ Megalohori ☎ 22860 81796 ⓦ www.vedema.gr

## PERISSA

**9 Muses ££** One of the better places to base yourself, this place is welcoming to families as well as couples. ⓐ Perivolos, Perissa ☎ 22860 81781 ⓦ www.santorini9muses.gr

**Meltemi Luxury Suites £££** Top-notch accommodation in Perissa: pool and pool bar, small fitness centre, airport transfers and a

lovely set of suites a short distance away for complete privacy.
ⓐ Perissa ⓣ 22860 83383 ⓦ www.meltemihotel.com

**Veggera £££** This small, comfortable hotel is a good choice for
families, with two pools for adults and one for children, a good
restaurant, and a choice of accommodation ranging from family
apartments and condominiums to luxury suites.
ⓐ Perissa town ⓣ 22860 82060 ⓦ www.veggera.com

### THIRA
**Hotel Galini ££** On the edge of the caldera at Firostefani, less
than a kilometre from Thira, the views from the bar are
breathtaking and there is a lovely sense of privacy about the
place. ⓐ Thira ⓣ 22860 22095 ⓦ www.hotelgalini.gr

● *The beautiful pool at Vedema Resort, Megalohori*

**New Haroula ££** Just under fifty rooms, attractively decorated and each with its own balcony. A small pool. ⓐ Thira ⓣ 22860 24226 ⓦ www.newharoula.com

**San Giorgio ££** Benefiting from the stylish Cubist architecture that so distinguishes Santorini, this hotel is in the very centre of town. ⓐ Thira ⓣ 22860 23516 ⓦ www.sangiorgiovilla.gr

**Hotel Porto Carra ££–£££** Comfortable rooms, with fridge and air-conditioning, facing the caldera, and has a neat terrace café for gazing at the panoramic views. ⓐ Thira ⓣ 22860 22979 ⓦ www.hotelportocarra.com

**Pelican ££–£££** Well-managed complex and every bedroom has free wi-fi. ⓐ Thira ⓣ 22860 22220 ⓦ www.pelican.gr

**Cori Rigas Apartments £££** A traditional house, over two centuries old, beautifully restored to create three suites and three studios. The terraces have soul-stirring views over the caldera and there is an arty little café for breakfast. An exquisite place to stay. ⓐ Thira ⓣ 22860 25251 ⓦ www.coririgas.com

**Hotel Atlantis £££** Rates depend on the type of room (with/without a balcony; facing the sea/village) and the time of year. A large hotel with a living room, bar, breakfast room but no restaurant, pool with whirlpool and situated right in the centre of town. ⓐ Thira ⓣ 22860 22232 ⓦ www.atlantishotel.gr

**Kallisti Thera £££** Close to the highest point of town, Kallisti Thera has the compulsory soaring view of the caldera, a lovely pool, and very attractive rooms (all in white) at a surprisingly affordable price. ⓐ Thira town ⓣ 22860 22317 ⓦ www.kallistitherahotel.com

# Preparing to go

## GETTING THERE
### By air
Charter airlines including Thomas Cook Airlines
(⟨w⟩ www.thomascookairlines.co.uk) and Thomson
(⟨w⟩ www.thomsonflights.co.uk) fly direct to Santorini from
London Gatwick and from a number of other UK cities from
mid-April until the end of October. Flight time from London is
around 3hr 30mins. There are also connecting flights from via
Athens with Aegean Airlines (⟨w⟩ www.aegeanairlines.com)
and Olympic Airlines (⟨w⟩ www.olympicair.com). easyJet
(⟨w⟩ www.easyjet.com) and British Airways (⟨w⟩ www.ba.com) also
fly to Athens. There are also internal flights between Santorini
and Greece's second city, Thessaloniki.

Many people are aware that air travel emits $CO_2$, which
contributes to climate change. You may be interested in the
possibility of lessening the environmental impact of your flight
through the charity Climate Care, which offsets your $CO_2$ by
funding environmental projects around the world. Visit
⟨w⟩ www.jpmorganclimatecare.com

### By ferry
There are ferries at least daily (sometimes overnight) between
Santorini and Piraeus, the port of Athens and several times
weekly between Santorini and other islands in the Cyclades
group, including Naxos, Paros and Mykonos, as well as Kos in the
Dodecanese and Heraklion on Crete. See the website
www.gtp.gr for timetables and reservations on all Greek
ferries. The fastest ferry crossing between Crete and Santorini
takes less than two hours, so flying to Heraklion (with Thomas
Cook, Thomson or easyJet, see above) can sometimes be a
better and quicker option than taking a connecting flight
via Athens.

## TOURISM AUTHORITY

**The Greek National Tourist Office** ⓐ 4 Conduit St, London W1S 2DJ ⓣ 020 7495 9300 ⓦ www.visitgreece.gr. Santorini's official website can be found at ⓦ www.santorini.com

## BEFORE YOU LEAVE

There is nothing by way of necessary inoculations that you have to organise before your departure, but it may be sensible to check that you are up to date with a tetanus shot. A small first-aid kit is advisable, even if it only consists of headache and stomach ache pills, a few plasters and an antiseptic cream. Note that codeine is banned in Greece. If you need to take medication containing codeine, bring your prescription. Be sure to bring sun cream, possibly some insect repellent and any prescription medication that is necessary. Pack your EHIC (European Health Insurance Card ⓣ 0845 606 2030 ⓦ www.ehic.org.uk). Adequate travel insurance and health insurance including medical evacuation and repatriation cover is absolutely essential. If you plan to rent a car or motorcycle, it is advisable to have insurance which includes legal liability cover and legal aid.

## HEALTH INSURANCE

Your EHIC will cover you for free – or reduced-cost – medical care at the Greek equivalent of NHS hospitals, but this will not include the cost of drugs or any special tests that may be necessary. Private hospitals and private doctors will offer a better service and if you have health insurance this will cover all the costs, including repatriation, if necessary; but be sure to keep all receipts and details of any medicines paid for. Having travel insurance will also cover you for the loss of possessions while on holiday.

## ENTRY FORMALITIES

A passport, valid for at least six months, is the one essential document you need. Contact the Passport Agency (☎ 0870 521 0410 ⓦ www.ips.gov.uk) well in advance if your passport needs updating. Holders of EU passports can stay as long as they like in any part of Greece. Many holders of non-EU passports, including Americans, Australians, New Zealanders and Canadians, can stay for up to 90 days without the need for a visa.

Pack your driving licence if you're planning to hire a motorbike or car and consider keeping photocopies of your passport and licence.

There are no customs restrictions for EU citizens.

## MONEY

The currency is the euro (€), pronounced *evro* in Greece, divided into 100 cents. For current exchange rates, see ⓦ www.oanda.com. Euro notes usually come in denominations of 5, 10, 20, 50, 100 and 200. Five-hundred euro notes do exist but are not common. Coins come in denominations of 1, 2, 5, 10, 20, 50 cents and 1 and 2 euros.

ATMs are available at most of the island's resorts. Credit cards are accepted in many places, and all but small shops and budget restaurants will take them. The use of a credit card will be essential if hiring a car or buying an airline ticket.

An ATM card should suffice for your stay, but it is advisable to have a backup, by way of either a second ATM card for another bank, sterling or euro cash, or traveller's cheques. A commission is charged for traveller's cheques so avoid ordering lots of small-value ones. In an emergency, money can be wired from your home bank; and see ⓦ www.moneygram.com ⓦ www.westernunion.com. Keep a separate record of any traveller's cheque numbers and the relevant bank telephone numbers if you need to report a lost or stolen card.

## CLIMATE

The warm months are between May and October, and the hottest, when temperatures average 25°C (76°F), are July and August. The only surprise in summer is the *meltémi*, a strong, hot, northerly gale that can blow for three days at a time, making it dangerous to swim and unpleasant to sunbathe on the beach.

July and August are very busy as well as very hot months on Santorini and this brings maximum enjoyment to some visitors; others prefer the gentler warmth of spring or autumn. If you want to avoid the crowds then the ideal time to visit Santorini is from mid-September to mid-October. During this time the sea is still warm enough for swimming, the climate is hot enough for sunbathing and acquiring a tan, and the traffic levels low enough to make parking rarely a problem. By the end of October many of the bars and restaurants in the resorts have closed down for the season.

In summer, pack only light clothing but allow for a long-sleeved garment and trousers in case you do suffer from the sun; in spring or autumn, include a light jumper for the occasional chilly evening.

## BAGGAGE ALLOWANCE

More restrictive airline baggage allowances and tighter airport security rules mean it is important to plan your packing carefully. Only one piece of carry-on luggage is permitted at British airports, and liquids, gels, creams and ointments may be taken through airport security checks only in containers holding less than 100 ml. Items such as cameras, laptops and handbags must travel in your single carry-on bag. Checked (or hold) baggage allowances vary from airline to airline, so it is essential to check your allowance with your airline before you start packing. As a rough guideline, the carry-on allowance may be as low as 5 kg (11 lb) and the checked-in luggage allowance as low as 15 kg (33 lb). Some airlines now charge for any checked-in luggage.

# During your stay

### AIRPORTS

Santorini's airport (☎ 22860 28400) is on the east side of the island, north of Kamari and a short way south of Monolithos. A shuttle-bus runs regularly, until 22.00, between the airport and the bus station in Thira, but unless you are staying close to Thira you will need to take a taxi to your accommodation. Most resort hotels arrange transport to and from the airport for their guests but this should be confirmed before you leave. Car hire desks are open for arriving flights, but every resort has numerous places for hiring vehicles.

### COMMUNICATIONS
### Telephones

Public card phones can be found in all the resort areas, and phone cards (*telekártes*) are readily available from kiosks and mini-markets. For international calls, purchase a *Khronokarta* that is issued by OTE (the main telephone company) or one of

> **TELEPHONING GREECE**
> To phone Greece from abroad, dial 00 + 30 (Greece's international code) + the full ten-digit local number.
>
> **TELEPHONING ABROAD**
> To phone abroad from Greece, dial 00 + the country code (44 for the UK; 1 for USA; 61 for Australia; 353 for Ireland ) + the number (dropping the initial zero of the local code for the UK and some other countries).
> **Useful numbers**
> Domestic operator: 166
> International operator: 139/161
> (See also Emergencies box on page 118)

the various alternatives available from rival companies.
For local calls, you can also use coin-operated phones that
are found in hotel lobbies and bars. Greek telephone numbers
have ten digits (beginning with 2 if a landline or 6 for a mobile)
and all ten are rung, whether dialling locally or from abroad.

## Mobile phones
Your mobile phone should be able to make and receive calls
and text messages to and from your home country. If coming
from an EU country, roaming rates are now regulated and
more reasonably priced than ever before. If you're using a
pay-as-you-go phone, make sure you have topped up with
sufficient credit before departure.

## Internet and email
Most hotels will have internet access for the use of their guests.
Internet cafés are common in all the resorts, though they are not
so common in Ia, and their rates (usually around €1 for half an
hour) are invariably cheaper than those charged by hotels.

## Post offices
Post offices open 07.30–14.00 Mon–Fri. As well as inland and
international post services, express service and registered post
are also available. Postboxes are yellow in colour; express boxes
are red. Slots marked *esoterikó* are for domestic mail while
those marked *exoterikó* are for overseas mail. Main post offices
are found in Thira, Ia and Emborio and smaller ones in Kamari
and Perissa. Many shops selling postcards will retail stamps as
well and many hotels will post mail for their guests.

## CUSTOMS
There are no special customs that the visitor needs to be aware
of. The residents of Santorini are well used to holidaymakers, but
this does not mean they tolerate outrageous behaviour and the

police can be quick to arrest anyone seen to be acting in an obviously obnoxious or lewd manner. Inebriety is not accepted as an excuse.

When out walking, bear in mind that zebra crossings do not give pedestrians an automatic right to cross, and care should always be taken when crossing roads; a local driver may flash headlights as an invitation to cross or a warning not to; and, when about to cross a road or a busy junction, always remember that driving is on the right.

## DRESS CODES

There are no dress codes as such but the better restaurants and bars do not expect customers to be dressed in beach attire, especially at night. Nude bathing is not legal but the western side of the secluded Koloumbo beach, on the northeast coast of Santorini, is popular with nudists and recognised as such. Note that when visiting a building of religious importance here, shoulders and legs should be covered as a sign of respect.

## ELECTRICITY

The voltage is 220 V (50 hertz). The usual type of plug in Greece has two round pins, so bring your own adaptor if your appliance comes fitted with a three-pin plug. Appliances for use in North America, using 110 or 120 volts, will require a step-down transformer.

**EMERGENCIES**
**Telephone numbers**
**Ambulance** 166
**Fire** 199 or the local number ☎ 22860 25812
**Hospital** ☎ 22860 23123
**Police** 100, 112 or the local number ☎ 22860 22649

**Consulates & embassies in Athens**
**Ireland** 7 Vass. Konstantinou ☎ 21072 32771
**UK** 1 Ploutárchou St ☎ 21072 72600
**USA** Vass. Sofias ☎ 21072 12951

If you have a health problem and need medical attention, contact the Santorini Health Centre in Thira (☎ 22860 23123 🕐 09.00–14.00, 18.00–21.00 Mon–Fri, closed Sat & Sun) or ask your hotel reception for the number of a local private doctor. The Zacharopoulos Pharmacy (☎ 22860 23444), next to the main square in Thira, has a reasonable stock of medicines, and staff can provide some basic advice for common ailments. If closed, one of the other pharmacies in Thira will be open at weekends and at night; emergency phone numbers are usually posted on the doors of pharmacies. A red Maltese cross marks the location of a pharmacy. A list of local dentists, doctors and pharmacies can also be found at ⓦ www.santorini.net

## GETTING AROUND
Santorini is a small island and no long journeys are necessary once you have arrived. There are useful bus services and these, supplemented by taxis, will meet many of your needs. Motorbikes, scooters and cars are available for hire, but the roads become very busy in the summer and finding a parking space can be difficult, especially in Thira and Ia.

### Public transport
Buses connect Thira with all the main resort areas and in the summer months they run into the early hours of the morning. Always keep your ticket because inspectors do make spot checks. To confirm schedules ☎ 22860 25404 ⓦ www.ktel-santorini.gr and bear in mind that buses are less frequent at weekends.

### Taxis

Taxis are relatively expensive and expect to pay, for example, €15 for a trip from one of the beach resort areas to Thira. There are a number of taxi companies and bookings can be made by phone.
☎ 22860 22555/22860 22869/22860 23951

### Hiring a car

There are a number of companies whose conditions of hire can be checked online and their rates compared. The minimum age for car hire is 21 years old. Try Drossos Rent a Car ☎ 22860 71492 Ⓦ www.drossos.gr and Sun Time ☎ 22860 25490 Ⓦ www.suntime.gr as well as international car hire companies. At all the resorts it is easy to hire large-wheeled motorbikes that are fun to ride.

Check carefully the conditions of vehicle hire, especially with regard to the level of insurance being provided, and ensure that you know what to do in the event of a breakdown. Usually, you need to pay extra to ensure full insurance cover. You will also need to show your driving licence, and travellers from non-EU states will need an International Driving Permit. You may also need to provide a credit card so that a deposit can be taken.

### HEALTH, SAFETY & CRIME

It is advisable to use bottled water for drinking, although tap water can be used safely for cleaning your teeth. Around Ia, the tap water comes from a local desalination plant and is considered safe for drinking, but it is best to stick to bottled water nevertheless. However careful you are, a bout of diarrhoea is a holiday hazard in Greece and it is not a bad idea to add some tablets for this in your first-aid kit. Such medicine is also available from pharmacies and for minor ailments a visit to one is often sufficient. Pharmacists speak English and can dispense drugs that in the UK would require a prescription. An English-speaking doctor should be consulted if the pharmacist advises or if you feel it is necessary. See Emergencies box on page 118 for the number of the hospital on Santorini.

Beware of the danger of exposing yourself for too long to the sun, especially in the first few days, and drink far more water than you would usually.

Personal safety is not something to worry about unduly on Santorini – Greece is generally a safe country and Santorini is one of the safest islands you could visit. Even at 02.00 or 03.00 it is generally safe to travel down the dark and narrow cobbled laneways of Thira and Ia. Sensible precautions, however, should be taken with regards to personal possessions. The law requires that some form of suitable ID is carried at all times and a passport or driving licence fulfils this need. If any of your possessions are stolen, be sure to make a report to the local police and obtain some verification, as this will almost

## DRIVING ON SANTORINI

Drive on the right side of the road and observe the speed limits that are indicated by the side of the road; speed traps are not uncommon, especially on the north coast road. If stopped for any reason, you need to be able to produce your licence, passport and vehicle hire contract. The No Parking sign is a blue circle with a red border and a diagonal cross. Beware of other drivers because the roads are very busy in the summer and impatient drivers will overtake suddenly, often without indicating. Local drivers flash their headlights for a variety of reasons, often to indicate they want you to pull over and let them overtake.

The roads on Santorini are not wide and rarely straight for any great length. This can become frustrating if you are driving a car and get stuck behind slower traffic such as buses, lorries or quad bikes.

certainly be required if you make a claim on your travel insurance policy.

## MEDIA

Newspapers from Britain are available, though there is a price supplement and a Sunday paper will cost at least €4. The larger resorts will have the widest selection, though you may be reading yesterday's news because of the time it takes for newspapers to reach the island. English-language magazines tend to be restricted to *Time* and *Newsweek*. There is a weekly English-language newspaper, the *Athens News*, which should be available at weekends and this can also be read online at Ⓦ www.athensnews.gr

Depending on what your hotel has signed up for, you may have access to cable and satellite television stations with films and programmes in English. Every resort will have some bars with satellite television showing Premiership football and other major sports events. There are a number of Greek television stations, some of which occasionally broadcast Hollywood movies in English with Greek subtitles. On the whole, though, the television in your hotel bedroom will provide minimal entertainment value.

There are two local guidebooks that are available at no cost from hotel lobbies and tourist information offices – *Santorini Today* and the red-coloured *Santorini Guidebook* – but they mainly contain advertisements and general background information. The monthly and free *Santorini Times* is a small but useful newsletter, which carries bus and ferry timetables and practical information about what is on by way of entertainment around the island.

## OPENING HOURS

On Santorini, the kind of shops and offices that you expect to find back home will keep roughly the same 09.00–17.30 hours.

Privately owned shops and businesses that cater for visitors are far more flexible and, while some may close for a couple of hours in the afternoon, they will all be open by early evening and remain so until 21.00 or later. The opening hours for ancient sites and museums vary, and are stated in the text, and on Sundays the usual admission charge may be waived. Museums invariably close on Mondays. Banks open 08.30–14.30 Mon–Thur, 08.30–14.00 Fri, closed Sat & Sun.

## TIME DIFFERENCES

Greece is on Eastern European Standard Time, so is always two hours ahead of UK (Greenwich Mean Time) clocks. Put your watch or mobile phone clock ahead two hours as soon as you arrive and this will help ensure you don't miss departure times. Greek time is seven hours ahead of Eastern Standard Time in North America and eight hours ahead of Central Standard Time.

## TIPPING

Tipping is not obligatory. In restaurants, a 10 per cent tip would acknowledge your appreciation of the service. In taxis, rounding up the fare is a matter of course. It's good form to tip hotel staff if you've had outstanding service.

## TOILETS

Toilets in museums, bars and small restaurants are generally of an acceptable standard, as are most public toilets. Toilets in hotels are usually well maintained and the same goes for the better type of restaurant. It is not a bad idea to carry a small supply of toilet paper with you. If you need a toilet in a town, your best bet is to find the nearest good hotel. In Santorini, as in much of Greece, toilet paper is not disposed of in the toilet bowl and a foot-operated receptacle is provided instead. Signs advising you of this are usually posted in the toilets.

## TRAVELLERS WITH DISABILITIES

Santorini is a very challenging environment for wheelchair users and people with visual disabilities. Roads and pavements are potholed, access ramps are few, and many hotels are reached only by long, steep flights of steps. Drivers, even in built-up areas, are frequently inconsiderate. Access to ferries and excursion boats is difficult for wheelchair users. A few hotels do have some ground-floor rooms with limited wheelchair access, but it is essential to confirm what facilities are available directly with the hotel, as well as with your tour operator, before booking, and it is advisable to have confirmation in writing. You should also confirm your requirements in writing with your chosen airline before departure.

## A

accommodation 27, 37, 77, 108–11
Agios Georgios 38
air travel 97, 112
airports 97, 112, 116
Akrotiri 12, 71–4
Amoudi 18
Anafi 80–2
ancient Thira 13, 41, 74–6
Atlantis myth 11
ATMs 114

## B

baggage allowances 115
Baxedes 18–19
beaches 11, 12–13, 59–63 see also
    individual locations
    nudist beaches 19, 39, 79, 118
boat trips 13, 59, 64, 101
buses 27, 47, 49, 119

## C

cable car 49, 51
caldera 59, 65, 101
car hire 120
children 41, 98–100
churches 29
    Agia Irini 39–40
    Panagia Episkopi 29
    Panagia Katefiani 41
climate 115
credit cards 114
crime 121–2

## D

disabilities, travellers with 124
diving 101
dress 118
driving 114, 118, 119, 120, 121

## E

electricity 118
emergencies 118–19
Emborio 37–8
entry formalities 114
etiquette 117–18

## F

ferries 77, 112
festivals 29, 104–6
food and drink 84–93
    caper leaves 87
    cooking classes 52
    cuisine 86–7, 97
    drinking water 120
    eating out 84–6, 98, 100 see also
        individual locations
    menus 92–3
    opening hours 84
    ouzo 88
    picnicking 87–8
    tipping 86
    tomatoes 87, 88
    vegetarian food 91
    wine 13, 30, 31, 51, 67, 68, 70, 88–9,
        90, 97

## G

Gialos 77

## H

health 41, 113, 119, 120–1
history 9–10, 11, 71, 73, 74, 75
Hora (Anafi) 80–1
Hora (Íos) 77
hot springs 66

## I

Ia 12, 13, 16–25, 96, 108–9
insurance 113, 120
internet and email 117
Íos 77–80

## K

Kamari 12–13, 26–35, 96, 109
Katharos 18
Klisidi 81
Koloumbo 19

## M

Manganari 77, 79
Manolas 64–5
marriage ceremonies 106

media 122
medical aid 113, 119, 120–1
Megalohori 67, 96–7
Mésa Gonia 68
Mésa Voúno 74–6
Milopotas 79
monasteries
 Monastery of Zoodohos Pigi 82
 Profítis Ilías Monastery 68
money 114
Monolithos 61–3
mud baths 66
mule rides 47, 49, 51
museums, galleries and exhibitions
 21
 Archaeological Museum 49
 Art Space 30
 Exhibition of Wall Paintings
  from Thira 51
 Folklore Museum 51
 Icons and Relics Collection of
  Pirgos 70
 Koutsoyannopoulos Wine
  Museum 31
 Megaro Gyzi 51
 Museum of Prehistoric Thira 52
 Naval Maritime Museum 20
 opening hours 123

**N**
Néa Kameni 65–6
newspapers 122
nightlife 13 see also individual
 locations

**O**
open-air cinema 27, 31–2
opening hours 84, 122–3

**P**
packing tips 113, 115
Palea Kameni 13, 65–6
passports 114
Perissa 12, 36–46, 96, 111
Perivolos 37, 38, 39

pharmacies 119, 120–1
phones 116–17
Pirgos 67–71
post 117

**R**
Red Beach 59–61
Roukounas 81

**S**
safety 18, 41, 98, 118, 121
seasons 115
shopping 13, 20–1, 27, 94–7
 arts and crafts 96–7
 bargaining 95
 food and drink 97
 jewellery 95, 96
 opening hours 122–3
snorkelling 101
spas and treatments 20, 32, 42, 66
sun safety 41, 121
sunset-watching 11, 18, 21

**T**
taxis 120
Thira 13, 47–56, 95–6, 110–11
Thirasia 64–5
time differences 123
tipping 86, 123
toilets 123
tourist information 113, 122
traveller's cheques 114
TV 122

**V**
Venetian fortresses 21, 68
visas 114
Vlihada 39
volcanic activity 8, 9–10, 12, 13, 65–6,
 71, 73

**W**
walking 41, 49, 103, 118
water park 41, 98
watersports 31, 42, 79, 98, 103

## ACKNOWLEDGEMENTS

The publishers would like to thank the following for providing their copyright photographs for this book:

Bigstockphoto 22, 28, 33, 57, 72; Dreamstime T. Marek (page 25), A. Mcaulay (page 43), P. Cowan (page 50), J. Jarsák (page 69); Photoshot/World Pictures 12–13, 62; Pictures Colour Library 40, 46, 85; Sean Sheehan 5, 15, 19, 55, 60, 64, 76, 83, 89, 91, 94, 99, 102, 107; Superstock 81; Vedema Resort 110

Project editor: Tom Willsher
Layout: Donna Pedley
Proofreader: Karolin Thomas
Indexer: Karolin Thomas

Send your thoughts to
# books@thomascook.com

- Found a beach bar, peaceful stretch of sand or must-see sight that we don't feature?

- Like to tip us off about any information that needs a little updating?

- Want to tell us what you love about this handy little guidebook and more importantly how we can make it even handier?

Then here's your chance to tell all! Send us ideas, discoveries and recommendations today and then look out for your valuable input in the next edition of this title.

Send an email to the above address or write to:
pocket guides Series Editor, Thomas Cook Publishing, PO Box 227, Unit 9, Coningsby Road, Peterborough PE3 8SB, UK.

# Useful phrases

| English | Greek | Approx pronunciation |
|---|---|---|
| | **BASICS** | |
| Yes | Ναι | *Ne* |
| No | Οχι | *O-khee* |
| Please | Παρακαλώ | *Pa-ra-ka-lh* |
| Thank you | Ευχαριστώ | *Ef-ha-ri-sto* |
| Hello | Γεια σας | *Ya sas* |
| Goodbye | Αντίο | *Andeeo* |
| Excuse me | Με συγχωρείτε | *Me si-nho-ri-te* |
| Sorry | Συγγνώμη | *Sig-no-mi* |
| That's OK | Εντάξει | *En-ta-xi* |
| I don't speak Greek | Δεν μιλώ Ελληνικά | *Den Mi-lo (E-li-ni-ka)* |
| Do you speak English? | Μιλάτε Αγγλικά; | *Mi-la-te an-gli-ka?* |
| Good morning | Καλημέρα | *Ka-li-me-ra* |
| Good afternoon | χαίρετε | *He-re-te* |
| Good evening | Καλησπέρα | *Ka-li-spe-ra* |
| Goodnight | Καληνύχτα | *Ka-li-nih-ta* |
| My name is ... | Ονομάζομαι | *O-no-ma-zo-me* |
| | **NUMBERS** | |
| One | Ένα | *E-na* |
| Two | Δύο | *Di-o* |
| Three | Τρία | *Tri-a* |
| Four | Τέσσερα | *Te-se-ra* |
| Five | Πέντε | *Pen-te* |
| Six | Έξι | *E-xi* |
| Seven | Επτά | *Ep-ta* |
| Eight | Οκτώ | *Ok-to* |
| Nine | Εννέα | *E-ne-a* |
| Ten | Δέκα | *De-ka* |
| Twenty | Είκοσι | *I-ko-si* |
| Fifty | Πενήντα | *Pe-nin-ta* |
| One hundred | Εκατό | *E-ka-to* |
| | **SIGNS & NOTICES** | |
| Airport | Αεροδρόμιο | *A-e-rodromio* |
| Railway station | Σιδηροδρομικός εταμος | *Sidirodromikos Stathmos* |
| Smoking/ Non-smoking | Για Καπνιστές/ Για μη καπνιστές | *Ya kapnistes/ Ya mikapnistes* |
| Toilets | Τουαλέτα | *tualeta* |
| Ladies/Gentlemen | Γυναικών/Ανδρών | *Yinekon/Andron* |